1st EDITION

Perspectives on Modern World History

D-Day

1st EDITION

Perspectives on Modern World History

D-Day

Myra Immell

Editor

GREENHAVEN PRESS
A part of Gale, Cengage Learning

 GALE
CENGAGE Learning·

Detroit • New York • San Francisco • New Haven, Conn • Waterville, Maine • London

Elizabeth Des Chenes, *Managing Editor*

© 2012 Greenhaven Press, a part of Gale, Cengage Learning.

For more information, contact:
Greenhaven Press
27500 Drake Rd.
Farmington Hills, MI 48331-3535
Or you can visit our Internet site at gale.cengage.com.

For product information and technology assistance, contact us at
Gale Customer Support, 1-800-877-4253.

For permission to use material from this text or product, submit all requests online at
www.cengage.com/permissions.

Further permissions questions can be e-mailed to permissionrequest@cengage.com.

Articles in Greenhaven Press anthologies are often edited for length to meet page requirements. In addition, original titles of these works are changed to clearly present the main thesis and to explicitly indicate the author's opinion. Every effort is made to ensure that Greenhaven Press accurately reflects the original intent of the authors. Every effort has been made to trace the owners of copyrighted material.

Cover images ©History/Alamy and ©Everett Collection, Inc./Alamy.

LIBRARY OF CONGRESS CATALOGING-IN-PUBLICATION DATA

D-Day / Myra Immell, book editor.
    p. cm. -- (Perspectives on modern world history)
    Includes bibliographical references and index.
ISBN 978-0-7377-5789-7 (hardcover)
1. World War, 1939-1945--Campaigns--France--Normandy. I. Immell, Myra.
    D756.5.N6D18 2012
    940.54'21421--dc23   2011037075

Printed in the United States of America
2 3 4 5 6 7 16 15 14 13 12

CONTENTS

Allies have made the first of a series of landings on the coast of France.

and German claims of annihilation of British and Anglo-American airborne divisions.

CHAPTER 2 Controversies Surrounding D-Day

played a more prominent and decisive role in D-Day than the British. He maintains that this was due in great part to American mobility, adaptability, flexibility, and ingenuity.

CHAPTER 3   Personal Narratives

June 1944. He describes his frustrations, the problems he and his men encounter, and the actions they take before they realize the Allies have an edge and they must withdraw from their advanced positions.

Chuck Hurlbut

A US battalion member recalls what he did and how he felt on the ship taking him to the beaches of Normandy. He describes the excitement and tension of the landing and the chaos and catastrophe he encountered on Omaha Beach.

Ernie Pyle

A war correspondent describes the sights he encountered on a mile-and-a-half-long walk on the Normandy beach. He laments the waste, the destruction, and the carnage, and tells how the sight of German prisoners of war standing high on a bluff staring out to sea affects him.

FOREWORD

*"History cannot give us a program for the future,
but it can give us a fuller understanding of ourselves, and of our common humanity, so that we
can better face the future."*

*—Robert Penn Warren,
American poet and novelist*

The history of each nation is punctuated by momentous events that represent turning points for that
nation, with an impact felt far beyond its borders.
These events—displaying the full range of human capabilities, from violence, greed, and ignorance to heroism,
courage, and strength—are nearly always complicated
and multifaceted. Any student of history faces the challenge of grasping the many strands that constitute such
world-changing events as wars, social movements, and
environmental disasters. But understanding these significant historic events can be enhanced by exposure
to a variety of perspectives, whether of people involved
intimately or of ones observing from a distance of miles
or years. Understanding can also be increased by learning about the controversies surrounding such events
and exploring hot-button issues from multiple angles.
Finally, true understanding of important historic events
involves knowledge of the events' human impact—of
the ways such events affected people in their everyday
lives—all over the world.

Perspectives on Modern World History examines
global historic events from the twentieth-century onward
by presenting analysis and observation from numerous
vantage points. Each volume offers high school, early
college level, and general interest readers a thematically

arranged anthology of previously published materials that address a major historical event, with an emphasis on international coverage. Each volume opens with background information on the event, then presents the controversies surrounding that event, and concludes with first-person narratives from people who lived through the event or were affected by it. By providing primary sources from the time of the event, as well as relevant commentary surrounding the event, this series can be used to inform debate, help develop critical thinking skills, increase global awareness, and enhance an understanding of international perspectives on history.

Material in each volume is selected from a diverse range of sources, including journals, magazines, newspapers, nonfiction books, personal narratives, speeches, congressional testimony, government documents, pamphlets, organization newsletters, and position papers. Articles taken from these sources are carefully edited and introduced to provide context and background. Each volume of Perspectives on Modern World History includes an array of views on events of global significance. Much of the material comes from international sources and from US sources that provide extensive international coverage.

Each volume in the Perspectives on Modern World History series also includes:

- A full-color **world map**, offering context and geographic perspective.
- An annotated **table of contents** that provides a brief summary of each essay in the volume.
- An **introduction** specific to the volume topic.
- For each viewpoint, a brief **introduction** that has notes about the author and source of the viewpoint, and that provides a summary of its main points.
- Full-color **charts**, **graphs**, **maps**, and other visual representations.

- Informational **sidebars** that explore the lives of key individuals, give background on historical events, or explain scientific or technical concepts.
- A **glossary** that defines key terms, as needed.
- A **chronology** of important dates preceding, during, and immediately following the event.
- A **bibliography** of additional books, periodicals, and websites for further research.
- A comprehensive **subject index** that offers access to people, places, and events cited in the text.

Perspectives on Modern World History is designed for a broad spectrum of readers who want to learn more about not only history but also current events, political science, government, international relations, and sociology—students doing research for class assignments or debates, teachers and faculty seeking to supplement course materials, and others wanting to improve their understanding of history. Each volume of Perspectives on Modern World History is designed to illuminate a complicated event, to spark debate, and to show the human perspective behind the world's most significant happenings of recent decades.

INTRODUCTION

In April 1917 the United States officially entered World War I. Then US president Woodrow Wilson called it "a war to end all wars." Unfortunately, Wilson was wrong about that. In 1939, after the Germans invaded Poland, Britain and France declared war on Nazi Germany, and another major war—World War II—became a reality. Many never-to-be-forgotten events took place before that war ended in 1945. One of these was D-Day, the June 6, 1944, Allied invasion of Normandy, France. D-Day has been called one of the greatest events in modern history and the greatest amphibious invasion of all times. In the view of British historian Nick Hewitt, it was "probably the most ambitious military operation in history. . . . An operation of unprecedented scale, ingenuity, complexity and risk."

The number of troops and supplies involved in D-Day and the days immediately following are staggering even by today's standards. Consider the following numbers provided by the D-Day Museum in Portsmouth, United Kingdom:

- Around 156,000 Allied troops landed in Normandy on D-Day.

- 11,590 aircraft were available to support the landings.

- 2,395 aircraft and 867 gliders of the Royal Air Force of Great Britain and the US Army Air Force were used on D-Day.

- 1,213 naval combat ships, 4,126 landing ships and landing craft, 736 ancillary craft, and 864 merchants were a part of Operation Neptune, which began on D-Day.

- By the end of June 11, 326,000 troops, 54,186 vehicles, and 104,428 tons of supplies had been landed on the beaches of Normandy.

The preceding figures represent only a portion of the vast number of personnel, equipment, and supplies that were needed for the invasion. According to the History Learning Site, the overall plan included the movement of 3 million men in 47 divisions, moved by 6,000 ships with 5,000 fighter planes providing aerial cover. More than 100,000 men and approximately 13,000 vehicles were supposed to be moved during the first three days of the attack.

Small wonder that the planning and logistics associated with the operation were a nightmare, a challenge far beyond which any army had dealt before. All kinds of issues had to be considered. The element of surprise was essential for the invasion to be successful, so everything to do with the plan had to be kept secret. This meant that, among other things, the planners had to figure out how to amass an enormous amount of equipment, determine where to store it, and how to transport it—all without attracting any undue attention or arousing suspicions. The target for the invasion—fifty miles of Normandy coastline—was defended by the Germans. The planners had to find a relatively safe way to get onto the beaches from thousands of landing craft more than 100,000 men and 10,000 vehicles—all in one day.

The Allies knew they would need specialized equipment to deal with the terrain of the landing beaches and the lack of natural harbors needed to land people, equipment, and supplies after the beaches were secured. Starting several years before the invasion, both Great Britain and the United States began to develop new equipment to help fulfill the Allies' needs. One such piece of equipment was the flat-bottomed Higgins Boat. It was able to go right onto the shore and had a drop-down ramp front that enabled soldiers to run off the boat onto the beach and vehicles to be driven off directly onto the beach.

Another important machine invented for the Normandy invasion was the DUKW, an all-wheel-drive utility vehicle, part truck and part boat, commonly called the "Duck." It could travel through the water on its own power, onto the beach to deliver cargo from ships at sea, and right back out into the water to return to the ships. About 40 percent of the men and materials during the Normandy invasion were brought by Duck.

Still another specialized piece of equipment was the amphibious floating Duplex Drive, or D-D, tank, intended to get tanks onto the beaches quickly. Essentially a tank with canvas skirts that made it possible for it to float, the D-D did not need a harbor to get on land. Many other specialized tanks were developed as well. Known collectively as "Hobart's Funnies," each was modified to serve a specific purpose. One was the Crocodile, which, instead of having a main gun in front, had a huge flame-thrower that could shoot flames up to 120 yards. Another was the Armored Ramp Carrier, or ARK, which carried two ramps on its roof and, when parked with the ramps set in position, served as a bridge for other tanks to drive over.

One of the most innovative pieces of equipment developed for the Normandy invasion was the huge artificial harbor known as the Mulberry. The Allies knew that if they had harbors along the breakwaters just off the invasion beaches, they would not have to capture an established port right away to be able to supply the men moving inland. The Mulberry was their solution, viewed by one British historian as "one of the singular logistical achievements associated with the Normandy invasion." Within three days of the invasion, two Mulberries were built and operational, one for the US forces at Omaha Beach and the other for the British and Canadians at the French seaport of Arromanches. Each Mulberry consisted of a number of different components, including an inner breakwater made of hollow reinforced concrete six-story-high caissons, a floating roadway, and piers. Prefabricated in England, both Mulberries were towed across the English Channel and assembled off the invasion beaches. Ships deliberately sunk off the Normandy coast served as protection from the open sea. The Mulberry at Omaha Beach was destroyed by a storm a few weeks after D-Day. But the one at Arromanches, known as Port Winston, remained in use for eight months. In the first hundred days after D-Day, Port Winston landed several million men, one-half million vehicles, and four million tons of supplies for the Battle of Normandy.

Given the magnitude of the operation and all the issues and elements involved, D-Day planners knew that preparing for D-Day far in advance was essential if the invasion was to be a success. As a result, preparation began in earnest in 1942. In addition to the men and supplies sent to Europe to fight the war, from January 1942 until June 1944 the United States shipped millions of tons of diverse goods to Britain, including hundreds of thousands of pints of blood plasma, more than a million maps, huge numbers of cigarettes and toothpaste—and a replacement rail network. By the end of June 1944, close to 300,000 million tons of supplies had been off-loaded onto the Normandy beaches.

British factories greatly increased their production rates as well, working twenty-four hours a day to produce huge quantities of weapons, ammunition, and equipment for the invasion forces. An article in the June 9, 1944, issue of the *Winnipeg Free Press* applauds the efforts expended and the care taken by 280 British factories that, among other things, manufactured British and US tanks. Workers had to make sure that every rivet and joint was sealed, that each tank was tested in water up to the turrets and with the driver and engine compartments swamped, and that provision was made for air.

According to the article, more than 500,000 miles were logged by army and civilian trucks carrying parts from factories to supply depots that worked around the clock, seven days a week, putting together and distributing half a million components of five thousand different types. And, as the article states, for the Allies it was all worth it because "D-Day brought a great reward."

World Map

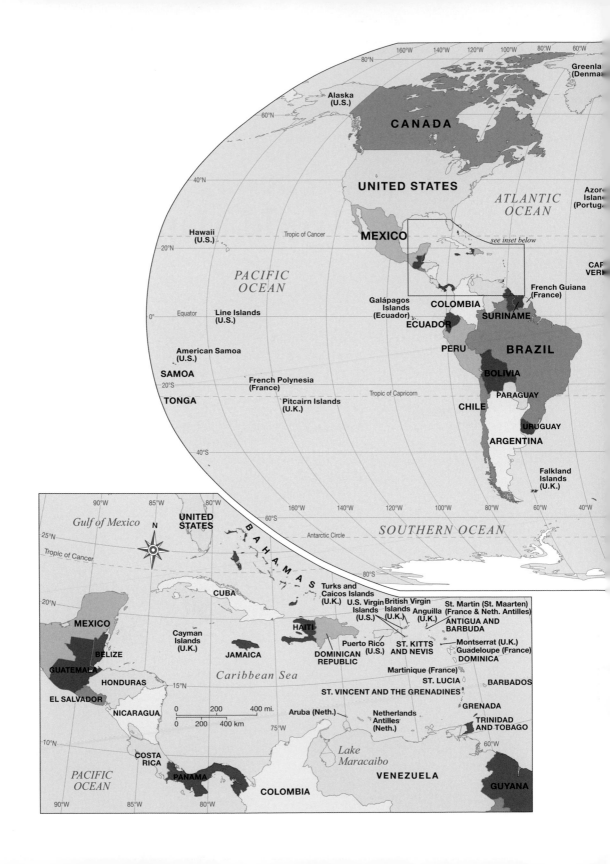

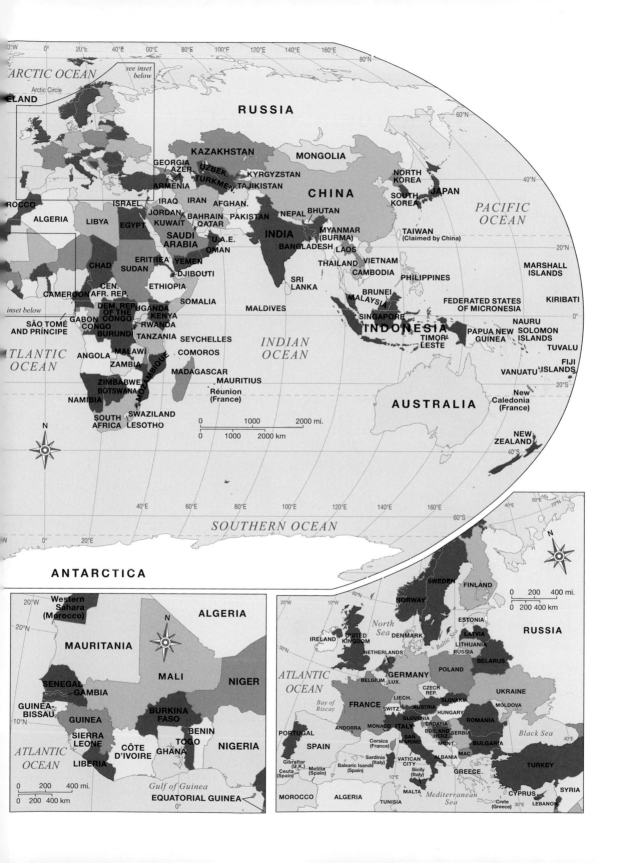

CHAPTER 1

Historical Background on D-Day

D-Day: An Overview

Encyclopedia of Modern Europe

The following viewpoint provides a brief overview of the June 1944 invasion of German-occupied France by the Allies—the United States, Great Britain, and Canada—and attitudes about the invasion in future years. Normandy was specifically selected as the invasion site, and steps were taken to help convince the Germans that the landings would take place elsewhere, the authors explain. The invasion was a huge undertaking for which an Allied air, land, and naval force began gathering in England six months before. Although the D-Day invasion was a major victory for the Allies, it was not one for the Soviet Union, which had wanted the invasion to take place several years earlier. Each year since the end of World War II, D-Day has been memorialized and continues to be celebrated as a symbol of the transatlantic alliance.

Photo on previous page: Soldiers in the US Army 1st Infantry division wait in southern England for departure to Omaha Beach on June 4, 1944. (**Galerie Bilderwelt/Getty Images.**)

SOURCE. "D-Day," *Encyclopedia of Modern Europe: Europe Since 1914; Encyclopedia of the Age of War and Reconstruction*, Charles Scribner's Sons, v. 2, 2006, pp. 780–784. From EUR 1914–2002 5V SET. Copyright © 2006 Gale, a part of Cengage Learning, Inc. Reproduced by permission. www.cengage.com/permissions.

T he term *D-Day* in general denotes the unnamed day on which a military offensive is to be launched. In particular, D-Day refers to 6 June 1944, the day on which the Allied forces invaded France during World War II, and to the following victory over Germany; in this connection D-Day stands for the greatest logistical achievement in military history as well.

Invasion Preparations

The preparations for the cross-channel invasion finally began after the Quadrant Conference at Quebec [Canada] in August 1943. On 18 December 1943 [US general] Dwight D. Eisenhower became supreme Allied commander and [British field marshal] Bernard L. Montgomery was appointed invasion commander. The plan for Operation Overlord, as the invasion was to be known, was for a landing in Normandy between [the French cities of] Cherbourg and Le Havre. The site was chosen for three main reasons: First, the coastline was favorable to a seaborne operation, with beaches and few cliffs. Second, the landing beaches were well in range of the Allied fighter airplanes. And third, the German army high command expected an invasion at the Strait of Dover, and therefore massed its most intact divisions, including all tank divisions, in that region. To further persuade the German generals that the landings would be made north of the Seine [River], the Allies created an entire phantom army, said to be based around Dover in southeast England opposite the Strait of Dover and commanded by [US general] George S. Patton.

In fact, during the first six months of 1944 the United States and Great Britain gathered an impressive land, naval, and air force in the south of England, the initial landing force concentrated between Falmouth and Newhaven. This invasion force consisted of five infantry divisions: two American (the First and Fourth Divisions), two British (the Third and Fiftieth Divisions), and one

Canadian (the Third Division). Seven more divisions were held in reserve. These troops were assigned to go ashore on beaches code-named, from west to east, Utah, Omaha, Gold, Juno, and Sword. Two American airborne divisions (the 82nd and the 101st) were to land behind the western end of the assault area, with one British airborne division (the Sixth) at the eastern end.

A Massive Number of Troops, Ships, and Aircraft

On D-Day, 6 June 1944, one day after the originally scheduled date, the Allies landed around 155,000 troops in Normandy; 57,500 Americans on the Utah and Omaha beaches; 75,000 British and Canadian soldiers on the Gold, Juno, and Sword beaches; plus nearly 23,500 British and American airborne troops. The troops had been delivered to the landing zones by an armada of nearly 900 merchant vessels and over 4,000 landing ships and landing craft, which had been marshaled and escorted by more than 1,200 naval combat ships. Some 195,700 personnel were assigned to the operation. In the air, nearly 12,000 fighter, bomber, and transport aircraft supported the landings, against which the Luftwaffe (the German air force) was able to deploy fewer than 400 planes. On this day, the Allied pilots flew over 14,000 sorties, and only 127 aircraft were lost. In the airborne landings on the flanks of the Utah and Sword beaches, more than 3,000 aircraft and gliders of the U.S. Army Air Force (USAAF) and the Royal Air Force (RAF) were used on D-Day.

> Some 195,700 personnel were assigned to the operation.

By the end of 11 June (D-Day plus 5), more than 320,000 troops, nearly 55,000 vehicles, and over 100,000 tons of supplies had been landed on the beachhead. Two weeks later, the Allied troops could fall back upon nearly 200,000 vehicles and 600,000 tons of stores. Most

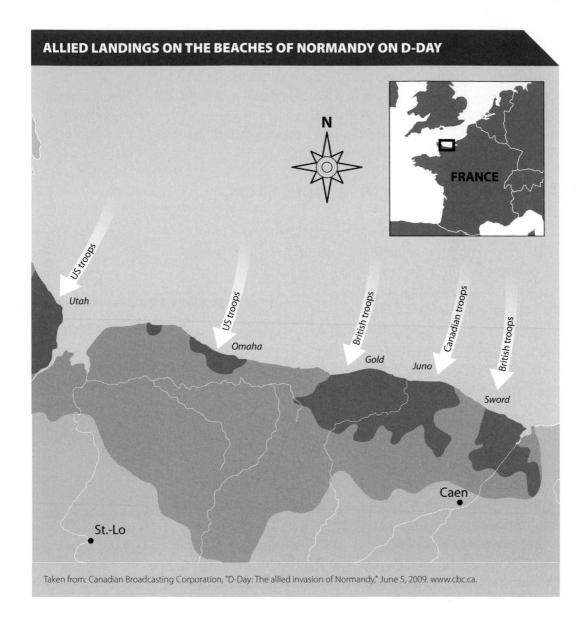

ALLIED LANDINGS ON THE BEACHES OF NORMANDY ON D-DAY

N

FRANCE

US troops

Utah

US troops

Omaha

British troops

Gold

Canadian troops

Juno

British troops

Sword

Caen

St.-Lo

Taken from: Canadian Broadcasting Corporation, "D-Day: The allied invasion of Normandy," June 5, 2009. www.cbc.ca.

supplies had to be landed on the beaches because the two artificial harbors, known by their code name Mulberry, were each the size of Dover harbor, and the five smaller harbors, known as Gooseberries, were not in place as scheduled. . . . Nevertheless, the enormous logistical effort not only enabled the Allied forces to land on the

Normandy beaches but also to develop an overwhelming weight of firepower, break out of the beachhead, and then fight and win a battle of attrition against the German troops. . . .

The successful invasion of the Continent on D-Day meant the foreseeable end of World War II in Europe. Logistics and reinforcements had been a major key to this great victory.

Troops come ashore a beach in Normandy, and Red Cross medics attend to the wounded, on the first day of the D-Day invasion, June 6, 1944. **(Popperfoto/Getty Images.)**

Resulting Attitudes About D-Day

D-Day and what followed was a great victory for the Western Allies, but not so for the Soviet Union. The former Soviet—and today Russian—attitude to the Normandy invasion has always been that the United States,

Great Britain, France, and the other Western Allies have never given proper recognition to the part played by the Soviet troops in the defeat of Germany and its armies. . . . The Soviets felt that they had been let down by their Western Allies. From the moment that the Soviet Union was attacked by the German Wehrmacht (army) on 22 June 1941, Moscow called upon its allies to open a second front against Germany. But it took three years before the invasion came off. When the Western Allies finally landed on the Normandy beaches in June 1944, the Soviets maintained that it was too late, and that as a result of this imprudent delay the war had dragged on and millions of lives, especially Russian lives, were lost unnecessarily. . . .

> It seems that today the memories of D-Day . . . are of more importance than the capitulation of Germany and the actual end of the war in Europe.

The French undoubtedly admired the stunning success of the Normandy campaign. They felt relief to be free but also a touch of humiliation that rescue had come from across the Channel. Being indebted to the Americans and the British for their liberation was, and is still, hard for the Grande Nation.

For the Americans, the British, and the Canadians, the invasion of the Continent was the beginning of the end of the war in Europe, and it seems that today the memories of D-Day . . . are of more importance than the capitulation of Germany and the actual end of the war in Europe on 8 May 1945.

Remembering D-Day

Not surprisingly, ceremonies commemorating the anniversaries of the Allied landings in Normandy were held every year. Usually, celebrating D-Day was a private event; some veterans of the invasion met in Normandy and remembered the heavy fighting. But in the later years of the twentieth century, the D-Day commemoration had become more and more part of world politics. . . .

D-Day has always had a special meaning for the Western Allies of World War II because it represented a huge common struggle, as President Franklin D. Roosevelt put it in his D-Day prayer, "to preserve our Republic, our religion, and our civilization, and to set free a suffering humanity." There have been, there are, and there will be (as in every relationship), differences between the United States and Europe, based on different views of politics, economics, culture, religion, and philosophy. But D-Day offers both sides a chance to put current differences aside. The shared commemoration of the Normandy invasion in which Germany, the previous enemy, is now included serves to remind Europeans and Americans of their common values and accomplishments. D-Day ultimately has become a symbol of the transatlantic alliance.

The Events That Led to the D-Day Invasion

Racine Journal-Times

The following viewpoint is an article from the June 7, 1944, edition of a local newspaper in Wisconsin and reported by the Associated Press. It provides insight into the background of the D-Day invasion and focuses on US president Franklin D. Roosevelt's D-Day statement. Roosevelt credited Soviet leader Joseph Stalin with the push for the opening of a second front in western Europe. The urgency of creating a second front in Europe was an issue as early as 1942. Roosevelt attributed the long delay in the opening of the front to a lack of arms. British prime minister Winston Churchill took a different tack in his D-Day statement; he focused on the future, announcing that the D-Day landings in Normandy were just the first of a series of Allied landings in Europe.

Josef Stalin [the Soviet premier] is spotlighted today [June 7, 1944] by [US] President [Franklin D.] Roosevelt as the forceful man who brought British and American leaders to agreement on undertaking the invasion of western Europe.

Careful examination of D-day statements by Mr. Roosevelt and [British] Prime Minister Winston Churchill reveal much of the background and some of the future of the great military adventures begun yesterday on the coasts of France.

Churchill chose to look ahead. In contrast with Mr. Roosevelt's D-day news conference parrying of forward looking questions on grounds that they were improper for reasons of military security, Churchill frankly advised the house of commons that more than one landing in Europe was contemplated.

Foretells Assault Scope

"During the night and early hours of this morning," he said, "the first of a series of landings of forces upon the European continent has taken place. In this case the liberating assaults fell upon the coast of France.... We hope to furnish the enemy with a succession of surprises."

That language sufficiently indicates the broad scale of blows to come.

> Mr. Roosevelt now expects the events and developments of the western front operation to demonstrate why the invasion could not have been undertaken a year or more ago.

The president dealt with the past, passing over that part of it in which he met with Russian Foreign Minister V.M. Molotov in May of 1942 for conversations which evidently convinced the Russians they had a second (western) front promise for that year.

Mr. Roosevelt now expects the events and developments of the western front operation to demonstrate why the invasion could not have been undertaken a year

Workers at a Firestone plant in 1943 make antiaircraft gun mounts and carriages. The D-Day invasion date was delayed because of equipment shortages. (R. Gates/Hulton Archive/Getty Images.)

or more ago at the demand of those then clamoring for it. That clamor came in its most vigorous and foreboding language from [the Soviet capital of] Moscow. It was echoed here in the communist and left wing press. To make his point, the president ridiculed the statement of William Jennings Bryan, secretary of state in the [President Woodrow] Wilson cabinet in which Mr. Roosevelt served as undersecretary of navy.

Lacked Equipment

Opposing the comparatively feeble armament efforts of the Wilson administration—the first order for 30,000 metal helmets was let only after we actually entered that war—Bryan held that 1,000,000 men would spring to arms overnight for the defense of their country.

What arms, the president asked his conference yesterday. He explained that it was lack of equipment that made it necessary to delay the opening of the western front so long and that men might spring but arms had to be made. Within a month of Pearl Harbor, however, he said, American military leaders and later the combined British and American chiefs of staffs were studying the possibilities of invading Europe.

> It was not until the Teheran conference . . . that the time and approximate place of the invasion was mutually agreed upon.

It was six months later that Molotov came here [Washington, DC] on a secret mission. As he left, the White House issued a joint communique which contained this language: "In the course of these conversations full understanding was reached with regard to the urgent task of creating a second front in Europe in 1942."

Agree at Teheran

When no European landings materialized, the Russians became angry and Stalin protested bitterly and in public. It was not until the Teheran conference last December, Mr. Roosevelt said yesterday, that the time and approximate place of the invasion was mutually agreed upon. In Teheran the three men—the president, the premier and the prime minister—finally got together. They then agreed that the invasion should come in the latter part of May or the first days of June. It was no more definite than that until very recently, the president explained, when D-day was fixed—June 5. Bad weather in the English Channel caused 24 hours of unforeseen delay. Only the actual date and the name of the commanding general remained to be decided when the three men parted at Teheran.

Eisenhower Chosen

One of General Dwight D. Eisenhower's prized possessions is a soiled memorandum written by Mr. Roosevelt to Stalin from Cairo [Egypt] three days after the Teheran meeting. The president and Churchill had agreed at Cairo, upon the man to lead the attack. The memo to Stalin read as follows: "Immediate appointment of General Eisenhower to command of operations has been decided upon."

Mr. Roosevelt smilingly pointed out at this news conference that since Teheran, there had been no Russian clamor for a second front but that, on the contrary, there had been every evidence of confidence in Allied military plans.

Prime Minister Churchill's D-Day Speech

Winston Churchill

In the following excerpt of a speech made June 6, 1944, British prime minister Winston Churchill informs the British House of Commons that Allied forces made a "liberating assault" on the coast of France. He reports that thousands of Allied ships have crossed the English Channel and airborne landings have taken place successfully behind enemy lines. The scale of the airborne attack is unlike anything ever seen before. According to reports, the massive and complicated operation is taking place as planned and the landings have been effective. Cooperation and unity is at an all-time high among the Allies, and there is utmost confidence in the Allied leadership, he says. Winston Churchill was a British soldier, author, and politician who served twice as Britain's prime minister and minister of defense.

SOURCE. Winston Churchill, "Sir Winston Churchill's D-Day Speech to the House of Commons," June 6, 1944. http://winston-churchill -leadership.com. Reproduced with permission of Curtis Brown, London on behalf of the Estate of Sir Winston Churchill. Copyright © Winston S. Churchill. All rights reserved.

I have . . . to announce to the House that during the night and the early hours of this morning [June 6, 1944] the first of the series of landings in force upon the European Continent has taken place. In this case the liberating assault fell upon the coast of France. An immense armada of upwards of 4,000 ships, together with several thousand smaller craft, crossed the [English] Channel. Massed airborne landings have been successfully effected behind the enemy lines, and landings on the beaches are proceeding at various points at the present time. The fire of the shore batteries has been largely quelled. The obstacles that were constructed in the sea have not proved so difficult as was apprehended. The Anglo-American Allies are sustained by about 11,000 firstline aircraft, which can be drawn upon as may be needed for the purposes of the battle. I cannot, of course, commit myself to any particular details. Reports are coming in in rapid succession. So far the Commanders who are engaged report that everything is proceeding according to plan. And what a plan! This vast operation is undoubtedly the most complicated and difficult that has ever taken place. It involves tides, wind, waves, visibility, both from the air and the sea standpoint, and the combined employment of land, air and sea forces in the highest degree of intimacy and in contact with conditions which could not and cannot be fully foreseen.

> I have been at the centres where the latest information is received, and I can state . . . that this operation is proceeding in a thoroughly satisfactory manner.

Success and Brotherhood

There are already hopes that actual tactical surprise has been attained, and we hope to furnish the enemy with a succession of surprises during the course of the fighting. The battle that has now begun will grow constantly in scale and in intensity for many weeks to come, and I shall not attempt to speculate upon its

course. This I may say, however. Complete unity prevails throughout the Allied Armies. There is a brotherhood in arms between us and our friends of the United States. There is complete confidence in the supreme commander, General [Dwight D.] Eisenhower, and his lieutenants, and also in the commander of the Expeditionary Force, General [Bernard] Montgomery. The ardour and spirit of the troops, as I saw myself, embarking in these last few days was splendid to witness. Nothing that equipment, science or forethought could do has been neglected, and the whole process of opening this great new front will be pursued with the utmost resolution both by the commanders and by the United States and British Governments whom they serve. I have been at the centres where the latest information is received, and I can state to the House that this operation is proceeding in a thoroughly satisfactory manner. Many dangers and difficulties which at this time last night appeared

British prime minister Winston Churchill celebrates victory at the end of World War II in London in 1945. (Keystone-France/ Gamma-Keystone via Getty Images.)

extremely formidable are behind us. The passage of the sea has been made with far less loss than we apprehended. The resistance of the batteries has been greatly weakened by the bombing of the Air Force, and the superior bombardment of our ships quickly reduced their fire to dimensions which did not affect the problem. The landings of the troops on a broad front, both British and American—Allied troops, I will not give lists of all the different nationalities they represent—but the landings along the whole front have been effective, and our troops have penetrated, in some cases, several miles inland. Lodgments exist on a broad front.

The Airborne Troops

The outstanding feature has been the landings of the airborne troops, which were on a scale far larger than anything that has been seen so far in the world. These landings took place with extremely little loss and with great accuracy. Particular anxiety attached to them, because the conditions of light prevailing in the very limited period of the dawn—just before the dawn—the conditions of visibility made all the difference. Indeed, there might have been something happening at the last minute which would have prevented airborne troops from playing their part. A very great degree of risk had to be taken in respect of the weather.

But General Eisenhower's courage is equal to all the necessary decisions that have to be taken in these extremely difficult and uncontrollable matters. The airborne troops are well established, and the landings and the follow-ups are all proceeding with much less loss—very much less—than we expected. Fighting is in progress at various points. We captured various bridges which were of importance, and which were not blown up. There is even fighting proceeding in the town of Caen, inland. But all this, although a very valuable first step—a vital and essential first step—gives no indication of what may be the course of the battle in the next days and weeks, because the enemy will now probably endeavour to concentrate on this area, and in that event heavy fighting will soon begin and will continue without end, as we can push troops in and he can bring other troops up. It is, therefore, a most serious time that we enter upon. Thank God, we enter upon it with our great Allies all in good heart and all in good friendship.

President Roosevelt Calls on the Nation to Pray

Franklin D. Roosevelt

In the following address made to the nation on June 6, 1944, the president of the United States tells the American people that the Allies are in the process of invading German-occupied territory— the beaches of Normandy in northern France. He asks Americans to join him in prayer. In the prayer he asks God to give strength and faith both to those at home and to the members of the armed forces fighting to preserve the American Republic and for liberation and justice. He urges the American people to devote themselves in "a continuance of prayer" to God to help their efforts. Franklin Delano Roosevelt served as president of the United States from 1933 until his death in 1945. He was the only US president elected to the office four times.

My fellow Americans: Last night, when I spoke with you about the fall of Rome, I knew at that moment that troops of the United States and

SOURCE. Franklin Delano Roosevelt, "D-Day Prayer," Franklin D. Roosevelt Presidential Library and Museum, June 6, 1944. www.fdrlibrary.marist.edu.

our allies were crossing the English Channel in another and greater operation. It has come to pass with success thus far.

And so, in this poignant hour, I ask you to join with me in prayer:

Almighty God: Our sons, pride of our Nation, this day have set upon a mighty endeavor, a struggle to preserve our Republic, our religion, and our civilization, and to set free a suffering humanity.

Lead them straight and true; give strength to their arms, stoutness to their hearts, steadfastness in their faith.

They will need Thy blessings. Their road will be long and hard. For the enemy is strong. He may hurl back our forces. Success may not come with rushing speed, but we shall return again and again; and we know that by Thy grace, and by the righteousness of our cause, our sons will triumph.

> We know that by Thy grace, and by the righteousness of our cause, our sons will triumph.

They will be sore tried, by night and by day, without rest—until the victory is won. The darkness will be rent by noise and flame. Men's souls will be shaken with the violences of war.

For these men are lately drawn from the ways of peace. They fight not for the lust of conquest. They fight to end conquest. They fight to liberate. They fight to let justice arise, and tolerance and good will among all Thy people. They yearn but for the end of battle, for their return to the haven of home.

Some will never return. Embrace these, Father, and receive them, Thy heroic servants, into Thy kingdom.

And for us at home—fathers, mothers, children, wives, sisters, and brothers of brave men overseas—whose thoughts and prayers are ever with them—help us, Almighty God, to rededicate ourselves in renewed faith in Thee in this hour of great sacrifice.

Many people have urged that I call the Nation into a single day of special prayer. But because the road is long and the desire is great, I ask that our people devote themselves in a continuance of prayer. As we rise to each new day, and again when each day is spent, let words of prayer be on our lips, invoking Thy help to our efforts.

Give us strength, too—strength in our daily tasks, to redouble the contributions we make in the physical and the material support of our armed forces.

And let our hearts be stout, to wait out the long travail, to bear sorrows that may come, to impart our courage unto our sons wheresoever they may be.

And, O Lord, give us Faith. Give us Faith in Thee; Faith in our sons; Faith in each other; Faith in our united

US president Franklin Roosevelt hailed the liberation of Rome (an Axis capital) by Allied forces during his fireside chat of June 5, 1944. (AP Photo.)

crusade. Let not the keenness of our spirit ever be dulled. Let not the impacts of temporary events, of temporal matters of but fleeting moment, let not these deter us in our unconquerable purpose.

With Thy blessing, we shall prevail over the unholy forces of our enemy. Help us to conquer the apostles of greed and racial arrogancies. Lead us to the saving of our country, and with our sister Nations into a world unity that will spell a sure peace, a peace invulnerable to the schemings of unworthy men. And a peace that will let all of men live in freedom, reaping the just rewards of their honest toil.

Thy will be done, Almighty God.

Amen.

D-Day: A Day of Surprises

Guardian

In the following viewpoint, the military correspondent for a British newspaper reports on June 7, 1944, that the D-Day invasion was postponed one day on account of the weather. The correspondent explains that, once the decision was made to go ahead with the invasion, minesweepers worked all through the night to clear and mark mine-free lanes, paving the way for more than four thousand Allied ships. Large-scale operations with airborne Allied troops went on all day. Surprisingly there were nowhere near as many German fighters in the skies as the Allies had expected. The *Guardian* writes that even though the invasion day landing operations were not easy, in some ways the German defenses in general were less menacing than anticipated by the operation's planners.

SOURCE. "Weather Held Up Invasion for 24 Hours," *Guardian*, June 7, 1944. Copyright © Guardian News & Media Ltd 1944. All rights reserved. Reproduced by permission.

There is a feeling of confidence at this headquarters to-night. No one imagines that the supreme battle which began on the beaches of Normandy [France] early this morning [June 6, 1944] will be won by the Allies without bitter fighting against a determined and desperate enemy, but there is a general sense that the "first hurdles" of invasion of the European Continent have been successfully surmounted.

The First Surprise

It has been a day of surprises—and the first surprise is that today should have been "invasion day" at all. For it can now be said that the operation which has been carried out was originally planned for yesterday. It was postponed on account of the weather.

When the time came for the decision to be made— "We shall invade"—there were clear skies and abundant promise of fine weather to come; but meteorological experts warned General [Dwight D.] Eisenhower's staff that the weather would change. This advice was heeded. Twenty-four hours later, when current weather seemed unsettled, the meteorologist forecast that to-day would be suitable. The supreme commander had then to decide whether he would trust the forecast or order a further postponement of the operation. He decided to trust the forecast. And so to-day the invasion began.

Weather conditions to-day in the [English] Channel and over the French coast have not been ideal, but they have served. Throughout the night minesweepers carried out the essential first task of clearing and marking "mine-free lanes," and in spite of a choppy sea and the necessity of working through a change of tide—their work had to be done in one night—they accomplished their task magnificently. It was the biggest, the most important and in many ways the most difficult minesweeping task in naval history, but these "little ships" cleared the way for the great armada of more than 4,000 ships that followed.

The Second Surprise

To-day's second surprise was in the air over the Channel and over Northern France. It has been calculated that the German High Command in the West can dispose of about 1,750 fighter air-craft, about half of which are single and half twin-engined machines. Probably well over 1,000 of these were in Germany before to-day's operations began, but there was nothing to prevent the Germans from transferring them to the Western Front.

In view of the extreme importance to the German High Command of repelling our invasion, it was expected that mastery of the air over the coast would be fiercely contested, but so far this contest has not occurred and Allied mastery is supreme and unchallenged. This morning some of our own fighters swept some seventy-five miles inland from the beaches to seek out German fighters—but they did not find them.

> "Between midnight last night and breakfast-time this morning something like 31,000 Allied airmen were in the air over France.

This is no time for conjecture and it would be folly to assume that great air battles are not yet to come, but it can be said that the scarcity of German fighters in the skies to-day has been at least remarkable.

Operations with air-borne troops have been taking place throughout the day on a very large scale and are believed to have been carried out with great precision. It is too early yet for reports from the ground to have come through, but it is known that casualties to aircraft taking part in these operations have been happily light.

Some idea of the scale upon which Allied air operations have been taking place can be gathered from the fact that between midnight last night and breakfast-time this morning something like 31,000 Allied airmen were in the air over France. This figure does not include air-borne troops.

Photo on previous page: A squadron of Allied planes flies over the English countryside on June 6, 1944, on their way to Normandy, France, where they found far fewer German planes than expected. (FPG/Getty Images.)

The Nazi Defense System

The Germans appear to have rested their main defence system upon the chief ports and to believe that while they control these no Allied landings can be sufficiently well established to enable a secure bridgehead to be maintained. The most heavily defended coast in the west is that on either side of the Straits of Dover, and next in order of strength are the Seine estuary and the [French] port of Cherbourg. In other areas the defences appear to have been developed later and to a lesser extent.

German artillery seems to be concentrated about the ports and to consist of four general categories—super-heavy, heavy, medium and light. The super-heavy batteries are either fixed or on railway mountings, and fixed batteries are often in strong concrete and steel forts. Concrete casemates are used, too, for ordinary heavy and medium coastal batteries, and important batteries are defended by a system of infantry "strong points," set up at intervals of about 1,000 yards but more closely together near ports and suitable landing-beaches. These major defence works are supplemented by an intricate system of mines, obstacles, and minor defences, and towns which the Germans regard as important are surrounded by anti-tank ditches and minefields.

> It would appear that the Germans have concentrated their defence on the beaches.

As in Italy and in Russia, the Germans seem to "key" the defence system to the particular defence of certain towns. Although certain coastal areas are heavily defended, these defences do not seem to be in any great depth, and it would appear that the Germans have concentrated their defense on the beaches.

Nothing at this stage should be allowed to give any impression that our landing operations to-day were easy; but it can be said that in some ways the German defences so far have not in fact proved quite so formidable as the planners of the operations had expected. The Allied naval and air forces have been magnificent in attacking heavy coastal guns which were menacing the landing parties. One American battleship went much closer in to the coast than had ever been intended to silence with her own heavy guns a particular Germany battery.

The German Supreme Commander in the west is Field Marshal [Gerd] von Rundstedt. He controls the ground forces through his own G.H.Q. [General Headquarters], naval forces through Admiral Francke, and air forces through Field Marshal [Hugo] Sperrie. Von Rundstedt's two army groups are commanded in the north by Field Marshal [Erwin] Rommel and in the south by Field Marshal [Johannes] Blasskowitz. It is Field Marshal Rommel in the north who is our immediate enemy; Rommel once more will have to pit himself against his old conqueror, General [Bernard] Montgomery.

The Germans have broadcast constantly to-day news of areas in which they claim that landings have taken place and inland, where they report Allied parachute troops and fighting. The Germans mention Barfleur, Carentan, and Caen as centres of operations, and they report Allied tanks at Arromanches, on the coast between Trouville and Grandcamp. They also report Allied paratroop landings in the Channel Islands. No comment on these German reports is yet available here. It is pointed out that the Germans frequently make such reports in order to "fish" for Allied comment.

Allies Advance from the Beachheads

Mt. Vernon Register-News

The following viewpoint is from the June 6, 1944, edition of a local Illinois newspaper and reported by the Associated Press. It details the Allied air and sea invasion of German-occupied Normandy in northwest France. They report that the invasion was a massive and highly coordinated undertaking that involved thousands of ships and smaller landing craft; thousands of American, British, and Canadian forces; and thousands of Allied bombers and fighter planes. According to reports from the field, it went according to plan and was highly successful. German resistance was not as great as anticipated and Allied losses among the airborne troops that led the assault were small. The Allies reported that the German air force reacted very slowly and the German navy had only a few destroyers and torpedo boats available. German radio, which began broadcasting invasion reports almost as soon as the first troops landed, continually aired news on the naval and air bombardments of the Allied assault.

The Allies landed in the Normandy section of northwest France early today and by evening had smashed their way inland on a broad front, making good a gigantic air and sea invasion against unexpectedly slight German opposition.

[British] Prime Minister [Winston] Churchill said part of the record-shattering number of parachute and glider troops were fighting in [the French city of] Caen, nine miles inland, and has seized a number of important bridges in the invasion area.

Four thousand ships and thousands of smaller landing craft took the thousands of American, British and Canadian seaborne forces from England to France under protection of 11,000 Allied bombers and fighters who wrought gigantic havoc with the whole elaborate coastal defense system that the Nazis had spent four years in building. Naval gunfire completed the job, and the beachheads were secured quickly.

> The Air Forces . . . estimated that between midnight and 8 A.M. alone more than 31,000 airmen were over France.

Allied losses in every branch were declared to be far less than had been counted upon in advance.

100-Mile Front

The Germans said the landings took place from [the French town of] Cherbourg [on the cost of Normandy on the English Channel] to [the French port city of] Le Havre—a front of about 100 miles, and that a strong airborne force was fighting as far inland as Rouen, 41 miles east of Le Havre.

Churchill told [the British House of] Commons:

"All this, of course, although very valuable as a first and vitally essential step, gives no indication whatever of what may be the course of the battle in the next few days and weeks, because the enemy will now probably endeavor to concentrate on this area."

He and all other sources agreed that the operation was going according to plan. The Air Forces, to which he paid high tribute for their work in smashing coastal defenses, estimated that between midnight and 8 A.M. alone more than 31,000 airmen were over France, not counting parachute and glider troops.

Battle at Rouen

The Paris radio broadcast a report that "a last-minute flash from the battlefield" early tonight announced "a vicious battle is raging north of Rouen between powerful Allied paratroop formations and German anti-invasion forces." . . .

An optimistic air pervaded this headquarters over the smooth manner in which was launched the great crusade to liberate Nazi-enslaved Europe, a crusade in which the Supreme Commander, Gen. Dwight D. Eisenhower, told his men, "we will accept nothing less than full victory."

Airborne troops who led the assault before daylight on a history-making scale suffered "extremely small" losses in the air, headquarters disclosed tonight, even though the great plane fleets extended across 200 miles of sky and used navigation lights to keep formation.

> The Allies had made good the great gamble of amphibious landing against possibly the strongest fortified section of coast in the world.

German broadcasts said the Allies penetrated several kilometers in between Caen and [the French town of] Isigny, which are 35 miles apart and respectively nine and two miles from the sea.

The initial landings were made from 6 to 8:25 A.M. British time (11 P.M. Monday to 1:25 A.M., Tuesday, CWT [Central War Time]). The Germans said subsequent landings were made on the English channel Isles of Jersey and Guernsey and that invasion at new points on the continent was expected hourly.

All reports from the beachhead, meager though they were in specific detail, agreed that the Allies had made good the great gamble of amphibious landing against possibly the strongest fortified section of coast in the world.

Reconnaissance pilots said the Allied troops had secured the beaches and were slashing inland, some of them actually running in a swift advance. The unofficial word at headquarters confirmed this, while the Vichy radio[1] admitted the Allied drive was going right ahead.

Unconfirmed reports said [German leader] Adolf Hitler was rushing to France to try his intuition against the Allied operation. Presumably, Field Marshals Karl Gerd Von Rundstedt and Edwin Rommel were directing the defenses from their headquarters in France.

Allies Land Tanks

German accounts through Sweden admitted that steady streams of Allied troops were continuing to land, particularly in the vicinity of Arromanches, about midway between Le Havre and Barfleur, and that tanks were ashore at several places. They said there was especially bitter fighting at the mouths of the Orne and Vire rivers.

The airborne troops' principal scenes of operations were placed by the Germans at Caen and Barfleur. The Germans said the American 82nd and 101st parachute divisions had landed on the Normandy peninsula, along with the American 28th and 100th airborne divisions. They said the British First and Sixth airborne divisions were operating in the Seine Bay area. The Germans complained that at some points dummy parachutists were dropped, exploding on touch.

Drive on Paris

If the Germans were correct about the locations, the Allied plan apparently was to seize the Cherbourg peninsula and make Normandy the initial beachhead for a drive up the Seine valley to Paris.

American Reaction on the Home Front

All across America that Tuesday, June 6 [1944], church bells were pealing; air-raid alarms sent up their mournful sounds; trains and factories blew their whistles; motorists zealously honked their horns and flashed their lights at one another. Through Hartford, Connecticut, there rode a man on a horse shouting the good news. But below the outward excitement there ran a solemn mood. Stores quickly closed or did not bother to open. Streets were generally deserted. Sports events were canceled. In cities, towns and villages the churches were packed with people—many of them hitherto unknown to local pastors and priests—praying and silently weeping. . . .

For the rest of the week there was a somber, religious mood. There was also a strong, if muted, sense of satisfaction. America waited patiently for once in a mood neither cocksure nor apprehensive. No one strayed far from the radio. Radio, in fact, was enjoying its finest hour of the war. All commercials were canceled. With the aid of shortwave, tape recordings and daring reporters it brought into American homes the

The German radio began broadcasting a constant stream of invasion flashes almost as soon as the first troops landed, and continued with extensive reports of the gigantic naval and air bombardments that covered the assault.

Announced 2:32 A.M.

Allied headquarters, however, kept silent until 9:32 A.M. British time (2:32 A.M. CWT), when the following communique was issued:

"Under the command of General Eisenhower, Allied naval forces supported by strong air forces began landing Allied armies this morning on the northern coast of France."

A high officer explained that General Eisenhower had kept resolutely silent until he was absolutely certain the landings had "taken hold."

authentic sounds of battle and vivid descriptions of the desperate fighting on the Normandy beaches.

In war industries absenteeism dropped to record levels. Factory loudspeakers broadcast a steady stream of news bulletins. Strikers went back to work. Red Cross blood donations soared. . . .

For one entire week the most boisterous, noisy, rambunctious people in the West went about with a restraint, a soberly responsible sense of purpose, that was not only striking, but without parallel in living memory. As an emotionally unifying, satisfying experience it was unique. It was the unity not of grief, but of accomplishment and hope.

SOURCE. *Geoffrey Perrett,* Days of Sadness, Years of Triumph: The American People 1939–1945. *New York: Coward, McCann & Geoghegan Inc., 1973, pp. 276–277.*

It was disclosed that a number of unannounced feints had taken place in the pre-invasion period, so that the Germans would not know when the real blow was coming.

96-Hour Air Attack

It came this morning as the climax of 96 hours of constant heavy air bombardment which reached a crescendo at H-Hour.

Warships of both the British and United States Navies, including British and American battleships, hurled shells into the coastal defenses which the Germans have been building for four years. The Germans acknowledged that this fire was tremendous and that it had set the whole bay of the Seine area afire.

The parachutists and glidermen went in after a personal farewell from General Eisenhower. The Germans said they landed at Caen and made deep penetrations at

> The German radio called it "a grand-style operation" both in area and number of troops.

many points, with at least four British parachute divisions employed besides the Americans and Canadians.

Great flotillas of minesweepers led the way to the beaches for the Allied ground troops, and the sweeping operation alone was described by SHAEF [Supreme Headquarters Allied Expeditionary Force] as "the largest in history."

German Planes Absent

The German air force reacted very slowly, although a high Allied officer said it had probably 1,750 fighters and 500 bombers it had been hoarding to meet the invasion.

The German Navy was represented only by a few destroyers and E-Boats [torpedo boats].

The channel was rough and there was a shower of rain at dawn. At Supreme Headquarters it was stated that the condition of the sea had caused some great anxiety, but that the troops had gone ashore, even though many were seasick.

The German radio called it "a grand-style operation" both in area and number of troops and admitted Normandy had been penetrated by the airborne troops "in great depth."

There was no confirmation from Allied sources of a rumor that the Caen airfields already had been captured.

Sea Battle Reported

Photo on following page: A business owner closed his shop on D-Day so that employees could pray for a successful invasion. (FPG/Hulton Archive/Getty Images.)

While the Allies described German naval activity as negligible, the Germans claimed a furious sea battle had developed off Le Havre between Nazi motor torpedo boats and the invasion fleet.

Low-hanging clouds and artificial fog with which the Allied forces covered the landings made it difficult to obtain a clear picture of the great assault.

BUCKLES
MADE WHILE YOU WAIT
WHOLESALE & RETAIL at LOWEST PRICES.
543
INSTALLED &RENTED
MADE WHILE -U- WAIT
Sorry
NO COVERED BUTTONS
MADE TO-DAY
WE ARE PRAYING
FOR THE SUCCESS
OF THE INVASION
NOVELTY COVERED BUTTON Co.
543-8th AVE
COVERED
MADE WHILE YOU WAIT
Wholesale & Retail
AT LOWEST PRICES

Allied sources said the parachutists dropped through low clouds, while the Germans complained that in some places dummies had been heaved over to confuse the ground defenses.

An Associated Press correspondent who flew over the scene in a B-26 bomber reported he saw hundreds of parachutes and gliders on the ground.

While making no effort to minimize the scope of the onslaughts, the Germans made their expected claims to have wiped out many of the airborne troops and to have scored hits on numerous warships and transports at sea. All these claims were without confirmation.

The Germans said their emergency reserves already had gone into action.

Tanks on the Beaches

Fighter pilots who returned from covering the first invasion waves said things already seemed well organized on the beaches.

"There was a hell of a lot of armored stuff on the beach that looked like tanks," said a Canadian flier. "I've never seen so many ships in all my life."

He and others said there was "lots of shooting going on" at the beaches but the troops got ashore well and many of the fighter planes did not even have to fire their guns.

A high officer at Allied headquarters described the landings as actually the third phase of the battle to crush [German leader Adolf] Hitler, the first having been the gigantic air assault and the second the offensive in Italy.

Civilians Warned

The air assault hit a new high today, with constant streams of bombers of every description dumping repeated loads on the chosen coastal area from which French patriots had been warned by Allied radios to withdraw at least to a depth of 35 kilometers (22 miles).

While the French thus were warned away from the immediate attack area, an Allied officer at headquarters declared, "we have high hopes of the underground in France which we have aided so long."

Ike Broadcasts

General Eisenhower broadcast during the morning an announcement to the peoples of Western Europe, telling them of the landings and declaring, "all patriots, young and old, will have a part to play in the liberation."

He urged against premature uprisings, however, saying, "be patient. [Prepare.] Wait until I give you the signal."

Note

1. Vichy radio was the radio station of the German-collaborative French government of unoccupied France during World War II.

The Allies Clear the Normandy Beachheads of Germans

Winnipeg Free Press

In the following viewpoint, a 1944 Canadian newspaper article relates what is happening in Normandy as Allied forces push inland from the beaches on which they landed on D-Day. They report that bad weather and greater German resistance have not impeded Allied determination or progress. The first real battles of the invasion have been going on in the hills and woods behind the coast. The beachheads have been cleared of direct German fire, and the first Allied casualties already are on their way back to Britain. According to German reports, their own armed forces have been strengthened considerably, and the German air force has been ordered to stop the Allied penetration at all cost. German forces have wiped out several British and Anglo-American airborne divisions and have taken Allied prisoners. According to Allied sources, their forces continue to resist successfully both in the air and on land.

SOURCE. "Allied Troops Fighting Inland," *Winnipeg Free Press*, June 7, 1944, pp. 1, 4. Reproduced by permission.

Allied invasion forces have cleared the enemy from all their beachheads in France and today were battering their way inland in stiff fighting after beating off the first heavy German counter-attacks in the Caen area.

The British, Canadian and American assault forces which stormed the beaches of Normandy were being reinforced constantly by hundreds of gliders and by surface craft sailing in to the coast from which the Germans had been driven.

Only one railroad bridge and five highway bridges were left standing over the Seine river between Paris and Le Havre by D-Day after Allied air forces had destroyed 25 railroad and nine highway bridges, Allied headquarters announced.

However, Marshal Rommel was reported in front despatches to be speeding armored and infantry divisions of the German 7th and 15th armies under his personal command to the invasion zone for a full scale counter-onslaught.

> Reports from the Cherbourg peninsula invasion front showed decided improvement . . . , and the Allies are making considerable progress on the whole front.

Both sides dropped air-borne troops into the framing battle front with Allied parachutists and glider troops pouring down early today from a 50-mile-long reinforcing sky train.

Fiercest Fighting

Paratroopers who spearheaded the attack by all accounts were involved in some of the fiercest fighting. The air-borne forces were revealed to have carried out all their allotted tasks, including the capture intact of several highway bridges which the Nazis had been expected to blow up.

The success of the biggest air-borne assault ever launched was regarded as one of the most satisfactory aspects of the invasion, which as a whole was considered in staff quarters to warrant sober satisfaction.

Reports from the Cherbourg peninsula invasion front showed decided improvement at midday, and the Allies are making considerable progress on the whole front despite bad weather and stiffening resistance, a headquarters officer said.

The invaders beat off sharp German armored counter-attacks in the area of Caen, 26 miles southwest of Le Havre and 9½ miles inland, where Prime Minister Churchill reported fighting yesterday.

By today they had cleared all their beaches and linked some of them, strengthening their overall position considerably.

The DNB news agency said the Allied beachhead in the Caen area was about 21 miles long, up to six miles deep at several points, and included both sides of the Orne estuary above Caen and the coastal strip to the west.

The first German prisoners, including coastal defence troops and survivors of the enemy trawlers sunk, arrived at an English port late yesterday.

(An Allied correspondent who witnessed the landing said the Allies had captured a 50-mile stretch of the coast to a depth of 12 or more miles, while a BBC commentator asserted that Allied bulldozers were clearing an R.A.F. airfield on the occupied coast.)

Front reports confirmed that British, Canadian and American assault troops and tanks—covered and supported by 11,000 planes and 600 warships—had firmly secured their beachheads along a 60-mile stretch of the Normandy coast of northern France between Cherbourg and the mouth of the Seine and were pushing inland.

A front despatch said Canadian forces, who landed between two British beachheads, were "ahead of schedule," and British troops and tanks were revealed to have seized a 25-mile stretch of the coast and to have driven inland nearly three and one-half miles to cut a coastal

An Allied Success Story

From the outset, the American airborne operations were bedeviled by confusion and bad luck. Three quarters of the 6,500 men in the 82nd and the 101st Airborne divisions were widely scattered by their flak-dodging planes and took no meaningful part in the action. One group of 30 paratroopers, from the 82nd Airborne Division, was dropped right in Sainte-Mere-Eglise—the town they were supposed to surprise. A trooper landed in the main square and was immediately captured. Another fell on the church steeple and hung there from his parachute pretending to be dead for two and a half hours before he was cut down and taken prisoner. Two men plummeted through the roof of a house and died instantly when the mortar shells they carried exploded. A German soldier confronted some French civilians and, pointing to the body of a paratrooper hanging from a tree, shouted triumphantly, "All kaput [finished]!"

But the paratroopers were far from *kaput*. Enough men had landed outside town to rally and take their objective. Even though the Germans counterattacked in strength, the Americans held the town and with it, command of the vital main road between [the French towns of] Cherbourg and Carentan.

SOURCE. Time-Life Books History of the Second World War. *New York: Prentice-Hall Press, 1989, p. 291.*

road over which the enemy has been moving reinforcements at several key points.

American troops had established themselves in one town, returning pilots said.

The first real battles of the invasion apparently were raging in the mine-strewn hills and woods behind the coast with the Germans training artillery, mortars and machine guns on the advancing forces from camouflaged positions.

Decries Over-optimism

An official spokesman disclosed that early reports of light resistance to the invasion actually were confined to the period immediately preceding the landings. As soon as the Allied spearheads of commandos, rangers and shock troops and engineers hit the beaches, however, they met stiff opposition.

> 'We've got through the defended beach zone and we have made it possible for General Montgomery to fight a land battle.'

Not until midday yesterday were the beachheads finally clear of the direct fire of the enemy, he said. He decried a tendency in "many quarters" toward over-optimism.

Admiral Sir Bertram Ramsay, Allied naval commander-in-chief, told a press conference last night, however, that the Allies had "broken the crust" of Germany's vaunted west wall.

"We have started off on the right foot and caught the enemy on the wrong foot," he said. "We've got through the defended beach zone and we have made it possible for General Montgomery to fight a land battle."

First Casulaties Streaming Back

The first troop casualties already were streaming back across the channel to Britain. A Red Cross train, six coaches long, carried the first wounded through East Anglia to base hospitals during the night.

German news agency despatches said the Allies had brought up "considerable forces" by ship and glider to a beachhead stretching from Caen, 18 miles southwest of Le Havre, to the coastal town of Bayeux, 22 miles to the northwest and 48 miles southeast of Cherbourg.

Massed formations of German operational reserves were concentrated on the perimeter of the beachhead

during the night and now were attacking with "terrific ferocity," Transocean said.

Another Transocean despatch said six battleships, 15 cruisers and 50 destroyers were supporting ground forces attempting to widen the beachhead.

Allied troops kept German POWs behind barbed wire in Normandy. (**Galerie Bilderwelt/Getty Images.**)

Annihilated, Say Germans

The DNB agency said two British airborne divisions were nearly annihilated in hand-to-hand fighting at Deauville, across the Seine estuary from Le Havre, last night. Four officers and 80 men were said to have been captured.

PERSPECTIVES ON MODERN WORLD HISTORY

South of Cherbourg, DNB said, an Anglo-American airborne division was "annihilated to the last man." Airborne forces which landed on the Channel Islands of Guernsey and Jersey also were wiped out the agency claimed.

Radio Berlin quoted the German high command last night as saying that "great fresh enemy formations had approached the French coast between Calais and Dunkerque, and Algiers later reported that the Germans had acknowledged the loss of an airdrome north of Calais to Allied troops. However, there was no confirmation of any landings except in the Normandy area.

No Opposition from Enemy Navy

Supreme headquarters in the third communique of the invasion reported that the Allies continued to land troops, guns, tanks and munitions throughout yesterday without opposition from enemy naval forces. Three enemy torpedo boats with an escort of armed trawlers had attempted to intercept the invasion armada as it approached the coast early Tuesday, but it was driven off with one trawler sunk and another damaged severely, last night's communique had reported.

"Air-borne operations were resumed successfully last night," the communique said without elaboration.

The German luftwaffe put in its first appearance in strength late yesterday, under an order from Reichsmarshal Hermann Goering to halt the Allied penetration at all cost.

30 Enemy Planes Shot Down

Twenty-six of a formation which attempted to interfere with heavy bombers attacking railways, communications and bridges in the battle area were shot down. Four more out of a formation of 12 Junkers 88s which made an abortive attack on Allied beachhead forces were destroyed.

While bombers smashed at enemy communications and other military targets behind the battle area, fighter-bombers and fighters flew low to blast and strafe motor truck columns.

A constant air umbrella was maintained "successfully" over the English channel and over the assault area, the communique said. Air losses yesterday totalled one heavy bomber and 17 fighters. Thirteen night bombers were lost. Night intruders partly offset the loss by shooting down 12 enemy aircraft without loss.

CHAPTER 2

Controversies Surrounding D-Day

The Invasion of Normandy Was Not Necessary

William F. Moore

The following viewpoint, excerpted from a research paper written in 1986, argues that the Allies did not need to invade Normandy to defeat Nazi Germany. By the end of 1943 the Russians had beaten the German Army on the eastern front, making it almost impossible for the Germans to stop them from moving forward to Berlin. Furthermore, by early 1944 US and British strategic bombing was systematically and rapidly destroying German war resources. The author states that both US and British planners of the invasion believed the invasion was a big risk that could cost many lives and possibly result in defeat for the Allies. The author concludes that an alternate British plan would have been the better strategy, but the United Kingdom could not dissuade the United States from its commitment to Overlord. At the time this viewpoint was written,

Photo on previous page: Adolph Hitler salutes his troops in 1943. He was criticized for not going to the Normandy front, which lead to division among his troops with no clear cut leader. (Topical Press Agency/Getty Images.)

SOURCE. William F. Moore, "I: Introduction; IV: Plans and Politics; V: Other Strategic Considerations," *OVERLORD: The Unnecessary Invasion*, March, 1986, pp. 1–2, 20, 22–23, 25, 27–28, 30–37. Copyright © William F. Moore/Air War College. All rights reserved. Reproduced by permission.

William F. Moore was a lieutenant colonel in the United States Air Force.

OVERLORD. Normandy. D-Day. June 6, 1944. The Longest Day. The event has been referred to as "The Mighty Endeavor," "The Great Crusade," "Much the greatest thing we have ever attempted," and other equally extravagant titles. Whatever the nomenclature, it commonly evokes the image of decisive victory—a do-or-die operation upon which hung the outcome of World War II in Europe. The common perception that D-Day, OVERLORD, was necessary, even vital, for victory against [German leader Adolf] Hitler has influenced policy decisions regarding the nature, size, composition, and missions of American armed forces from the end of World II to the present. . . .

This perception of OVERLORD is in all likelihood based upon an illusion—a myth. Americans typically believe that Nazi Germany was defeated during World War II by *American* fighting forces, and that it was primarily the skill and dedication of the *American* fighting man, the civilian-soldier, which proved decisive in this conflict. Typical Americans also believe that combined US and British forces were primarily responsible for destroying the German Army in 1944 and 1945 after the successful amphibious landing on the coast of Normandy. . . .

Popularly Held Views Are Inaccurate

Unfortunately, history shows these views concerning American and British supremacy and the importance of Normandy and the Western Front in Europe to be inaccurate. Operation OVERLORD and the massive cross-channel Invasion of Europe were not necessary to the military defeat of Germany. Furthermore, had the invasion merely been delayed for a few months, the political objectives which resulted from OVERLORD could have been attained with only a fraction of the British/American casualties.

These conclusions may seem startling or even ridiculous to those accustomed to popularly held views of allied victory in Europe. However, they are based on readily documented historical information. The historical record shows that by the end of 1943 the German Army had been beaten decisively on the eastern front and that it could not resist the increasing power and tempo of the Soviet advance to Berlin. It also shows that by early 1944 the American and British strategic bombing campaign was systematically devastating the German industrial base and that defeat or total incapacitation of the German war machine was inevitable—sooner, not later. Most remarkable of all, however, history shows that American and British planners believed that the massive Normandy invasion was not necessary to achieve military victory, and that it could easily result in a catastrophic defeat for the allied forces. Such a result would, as a minimum, have lengthened rather than shortened the war and could well have caused incalculable damage to the allied cause. . . .

> History shows that American and British planners believed that the massive Normandy invasion was not necessary to achieve military victory.

A Strong Lack of Agreement

Perhaps the most persuasive argument that OVERLORD was not necessary is the one that can be based on the intense disagreement that existed among allied strategists during 1943. The British consistently felt that a peripheral strategy based on operations in the Mediterranean and the Balkans was preferable to a large scale direct assault like the Normandy invasion. Although there was considerable internal support for the British recommendation among American planners, the official American

Soviet premier Joseph Stalin, US president Franklin D. Roosevelt, and British prime minister Winston Churchill (left to right) sit at the Teheran Conference discussing plans for the war against Germany. (AP Photo.)

position, as espoused by Gen. [George] Marshall, adamantly advocated OVERLORD. . . .

Gen. Marshall insisted that OVERLORD must have "overriding priority." If not, it, "weakened our chances for an early victory and rendered necessary a reexamination of our basic strategy with a possible readjustment toward the Pacific." To the British, this was the ultimate threat, since their hopes for a meaningful share in the defeat of Germany were totally dependent on continued American assistance. But Gen. Marshall followed up with a second body blow. He stated that a refusal to give OVERLORD top priority would result in his immediate resignation, a position he had previously expressed to President [Franklin D.] Roosevelt.

Although the Americans presented a united front at [the] QUADRANT [conference in 1943], it is interesting to note that a mini-revolt had occurred during the summer of 1943 among the strategists on the JCS [Joint Chiefs of Staff]. Led by Lt. Gen. John Hull, . . . these planners felt that a cross-channel Invasion was not necessary.

They recommended adoption of the British strategy of peripheral operations in the Mediterranean, continued strategic air operations against the German homeland, and continued use of dominant allied seapower. They advocated a relaxation of the total commitment to OVERLORD and advised against setting a firm date for it. . . .

The British, who had access to the same intelligence information as the dominant American war planners and considerably more experience fighting the Germans, felt that OVERLORD was both unnecessary and a terrible risk. With victory over the Germans practically in the allies' grasp due to successes in the north Atlantic, on the Eastern front, and in the strategic air campaign, the British saw no justification at the time of QUADRANT (or later) for risking an avoidable defeat which could have had catastrophic political consequences for the Alliance. . . .

A stalemate again existed between the American and British positions, and it appeared that [Soviet leader] Joseph Stalin would make the final decision by expressing his preferences at the summit scheduled for late November in Tehran. . . .

On November 28, 1943, the summit at Tehran began. Although Stalin had obviously been considering the alternatives, there was no question at Tehran that he preferred OVERLORD as the primary offensive for 1944. . . .

While [a "second front"] had been a consistent and well-justified theme from Stalin throughout 1941 and 1942, by late 1943 the urgency had been relieved. At Tehran, Stalin knew he could defeat the Germans unilaterally, if required. Although the possibility of a separate peace between Germany and Russia may have been a basis for real concern in 1942 and early 1943, by the time of the Tehran Conference it would have taken a catastrophic reversal to change the Russian commitment to victory. Russia was in the war to stay and to win. Furthermore, the Americans would have been well justified had they maintained that the second front already existed in the Pacific, where the Russian forces were not engaged. It may have been a great historical misfortune that the other allies could not do more to relieve Russia during the darkest days of 1941 and 1942 when she faced the Germans essentially alone, but this compelling need simply did not exist at the Tehran conference. By that time, the argument for a second European front was merely a "rationale of convenience."

A Devious Rationale

Some assume the allied decision to proceed with OVER-LORD was based on a desire to limit Russian territorial gains to eastern Europe. This rather Machiavellian rationale probably has more validity than a purely military one, but it also has several deficiencies. First of all, it was not apparent in late 1943 that Germany would fight to the bitter end. It was conceivable that surrender, rather than destruction, would be chosen at some point prior to Russian invasion of German territory. Occupation forces would then have entered Germany unopposed, and it is reasonable to assume that American and British forces would have been given preference. Secondly, even if the Germans did not surrender, continuing attrition on the eastern front would gradually have resulted in the transfer of German forces out of France, so British and American forces would have faced little or no opposition to a deferred landing there. . . .

> Even more opportunistic strategists would have recognized the wisdom of Winston Churchill's recommendations for a Mediterranean strategy rather than a massive invasion of France.

Even more opportunistic strategists would have recognized the wisdom of [British prime minister] Winston Churchill's recommendations for a Mediterranean strategy rather than a massive invasion of France. His strategy promised to do two things. First, it would have limited British and American casualties and risk, so that strong forces would have been available to confront Russia in the post-war world. Secondly, successful execution of this strategy would have prevented Russian occupation of much of eastern Europe. . . . Unfortunately, Churchill's mistrust of the Russians was completely ignored or discounted as an insufficient basis for changing the OVERLORD planning. It is therefore very unlikely that American insistence on OVERLORD could have been based on distrust of the Russians or a desire to limit their occupation of Europe. There were too many more favorable opportunities for doing this, had it been a strategic objective, and there is simply too much evidence to the contrary.

An Unnecessary Cost of Lives

As a final point on the strategic basis for OVERLORD, the potential gains from OVERLORD did not compare with its potential cost to the allies. . . . British and American forces could have been massacred on the beaches of Normandy or "Dunkirked" at a later date. This outcome is not only plausible, it came very close to actually happening. Repositioning one or two divisions would probably have given the Germans a victory on the Normandy beaches. Less interference by Hitler in the decisions of his commanders might also have given him a victory even after the allied beachhead had been established. The invasion was a serious and unnecessary risk. . . .

Having determined that OVERLORD was not necessary for allied victory in Europe; that OVERLORD was too late to provide the much needed relief to Russia; that OVERLORD was perhaps the least advantageous opportunity to limit the scope of Russian post-war occupation; and that as a strategy, OVERLORD had a greater potential for losing or extending than for winning the war; it is extremely difficult to justify the operation. The apparent

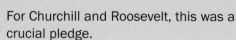

The 1943 Teheran Conference

On November 29 [Soviet premier Joseph] Stalin, [British prime minister Winston] Churchill and [US president Franklin D.] Roosevelt—the Big Three—met at Teheran [Iran], the Persian capital. Speaking of the post-war frontiers of Europe, Stalin told Churchill and Roosevelt that "the Russians did not want anything belonging to other people, although they might have a bite at Germany." . . . The Soviet Union would re-acquire the eastern third of Poland that had been taken by the Poles at the time of the Treaty of Riga in 1921—and subsequently transferred to the Soviet Union under the Nazi-Soviet Pact of 1939. Poland would be given a large swathe of east German territory in compensation, including the industrial region of Upper Silesia. Stalin also promised that the Soviet Union would enter the war against Japan "the moment" that Germany was defeated.

For Churchill and Roosevelt, this was a crucial pledge.

During their talks at Teheran, Churchill explained to Stalin that the launching of the cross-Channel landings would depend upon a "satisfactory reduction" of German fighter and military strength in north-west Europe during the coming six months. When Stalin asked if this meant that Churchill and the British Chiefs of Staff did not really believe in the operation, Churchill replied that if the conditions were met "it will be our stern duty to hurl across the Channel against the Germans every sinew of our strength."

SOURCE. *Martin Gilbert,* A History of the Twentieth Century: Volume Two: 1933–1951. *New York: William Morrow and Company, 1989, p. 532.*

basis for the final decision on OVERLORD was that the American strategists were committed to it. Even though the original rationale for OVERLORD was sound, American strategists refused to recognize that the European situation had changed. After fighting for OVERLORD for over two years with the British, the US Army would not relinquish its only opportunity to play a major role in the defeat of the Germans. . . .

According to [military historian] Trumbull Higgins,

> When the British were finally compelled by their Allies to invade France in 1944, it was an invasion essentially undertaken in the self-interest of the West, the terrible risk of the collapse of the Soviet Union having long since passed. At this date the Red Army no longer needed more than Western supplies with which to occupy eastern Europe.

The Normandy invasion was simply too late to be of meaningful assistance to the Russians. In fact, Stalin had conceded that is was no longer necessary.

Furthermore, many capable allied strategists knew that OVERLORD was no longer required and recommended against it. Why were these recommendations not heeded, especially since they would have resulted in greatly reduced British and American casualties? Two considerations cannot be ignored. First was the sheer momentum behind the OVERLORD planning. American planners had placed all their European "eggs" in this basket, they had been advocating OVERLORD against the British for over two years, and they were unwilling to concede to the British position in late 1943. Secondly, American leaders, including Roosevelt, felt that unless American forces took a significant (albeit late) share in defeating the German Army, the Russians would be entirely uncooperative in the post-war world and probably would not assist in defeating the Japanese. The British were much less concerned about Russian sensitivities, feeling instead that their post-war interests would be better served by strengthening and conserving their armed forces rather than squandering them on the beaches of Normandy.

Strategic Inflexibility and Parochialism

OVERLORD . . . was an unnecessary military gamble that could easily have failed. In retrospect, it is impossible to understand why American strategists were so committed to it. This commitment itself is evidence of serious strategic inflexibility. American planners either could not or would not adjust to the realities of the European theater in late 1943 and early 1944. Having already made the investment in a strategic bombing force that, in combination with the Russian Army, could have defeated Germany in a matter of months, why did the US not unleash the bombers and turn its attention to the Pacific theater? Why did US strategists not accept British recommendations for a less risky Mediterranean/ Balkan strategy that would have left the western forces in a much more favorable post-war position relative to the Russians? The answers to these questions have political as well as military dimensions. President Roosevelt believed he could buy Stalin's post-war cooperation. When Stalin expressed his final preference for OVERLORD at Tehran, he essentially allowed American political and military strategy to coalesce. . . .

In the final analysis, parochialism cannot be discounted. During World War I American leaders and forces had chafed under the constraints of a strategy developed by Britain. With World War II, America had another opportunity to assert its world leadership role and develop the strategy for victory. Gen. Marshall was entirely consistent with the attitudes of the American people and their political leaders when he insisted that OVERLORD, the American plan, would be used to defeat Germany. Furthermore, and perhaps even more important to Gen. Marshall, he knew that victory in the Pacific theater would be achieved primarily by Naval and Air forces. Geography alone dictated this. OVERLORD was the last opportunity for the US Army to play a major rather than a peripheral role in the victory. General Marshall simply would not let such an opportunity pass.

D-Day Was Not a Mistake

Gordon Harrison

The author of the following viewpoint, written in 1957, contends that the American plan to invade France was sound military strategy. He writes that the British had no political interest in the Mediterranean and that there is no proof that their proposed strategy was meant to discourage future Soviet aggression in eastern Europe. The British were not adverse to the American cross-channel attack strategy. Their hesitation arose from the fact that they were not sure the Allies would be able to carry it off. He concludes that the Allies' primary mission in Europe in World War II was to crush Germany, and the military judgment was that the best way to accomplish that goal was to fight in France. Gordon Harrison served as a wartime combat historian during World War II and in 1951 authored *Cross-Channel Attack*, the official US history of the Normandy invasion.

SOURCE. Gordon Harrison, "Was D-Day a Mistake?" *Harper's*, August 1951, pp. 77–81. Copyright © 1951 by Harper's Magazine. All rights reserved. Reproduced from the August issue by special permission.

An expert billiard player tries to make each carom in such a way as to set up the balls for the next shot. Our victory over Germany in World War II seems to have been a billiard by an amateur—brilliant after its own fashion but productive of nothing but trouble for the next play. Criticisms of the manner of that victory have been many but none more challenging than the charge that the invasion of Normandy in June 1944, leading to the surrender of Germany eleven months later, was one of our worst blunders. That victory at arms, it is said, was a political defeat. It was a defeat because it carried our armies into Europe from the wrong direction and left them politically useless on the banks of the Elbe [River], when they should have been blocking Soviet imperialism from positions around Prague [Czechoslovakia, now Czech Republic] and Dresden [Germany]. While our British allies, the critics continue, foresaw in 1942–43 the advantage of occupying central Europe

US Army chief of staff, General George C. Marshall, one of the planners and crusaders for the D-Day invasion, talks to GIs as he tours the beachheads in France. **(Hulton Archive/ Getty Images.)**

ahead of the Russians and therefore urged an invasion through the Balkans, American military leaders, blindly ignoring politics, insisted on the quick road to victory through France. The Balkan invasion was scrapped; we stormed through Normandy, saved a few fighting months—and lost the peace.

A Flawed Hypothesis

This hypothesis, most ably advanced by [*New York Times* military affairs editor and Pulitzer Prize winner] Hanson W. Baldwin in his book, *Great Mistakes of the War*, has the fascination of all historical "might-have-beens." In addition, it suggests as a general principle of war that strategists should provide not only for victory but for the maneuver of armies as political pawns in the postwar contest for power. It asserts that this principle was actually at stake in the 1942–43 Anglo-American debates on the strategy for defeating Germany and

> The hypothesis [that D-Day was a political defeat], for all its fascination, does not fit the facts.

was disastrously scuttled by the stubbornness of General [George C.] Marshall and the American Army.

The hypothesis, for all its fascination, does not fit the facts. It rests on what seems to me a serious misreading of history. I have carefully searched the written record as well as the oral testimony of a great many participants in and witnesses to the strategy-making and have found nothing to indicate that British strategy was ever aimed at frustrating future Soviet aggression in eastern Europe. . . .

The American Strategy

The allegations of British political interest in the Mediterranean were first made by American officers concerned with the planning for the Normandy invasion. What political interests were involved and who on the

British side was particularly motivated by them were not then specified. After the war the charges were repeated in writing by Americans who were on the fringes of the planning. . . . Significantly all these American interpretations of British motives prickle with irritation. That irritation is a historical fact of considerable importance, for it reflects the highly emotional atmosphere which surrounded the Anglo-American debate.

Early in 1942, Secretary of War Henry L. Stimson, General George C. Marshall, and the Operations Division of the War Department worked out a master project for beating Germany by a power blow across the English Channel, to be struck at a definite date dependent only on our own state of preparedness. The architects of this policy—Stimson, Marshall, and the army planners—became, as opposition developed, crusaders for it. The strategy seemed to them the only efficient way to victory. It perfectly fitted with the American military potential and with American impatience to end the war. They recognized that the cross-Channel attack would have to be mounted on an unprecedented scale, that it would take all the combined resources of America and Great Britain in excess of the minimum needed to hold the Japanese in the Pacific. They recognized that it would take time to prepare and above all an unqualified resolution to face the difficulties at the outset and to overcome them. Out of their conviction and their concern they developed a quasi-religious faith.

British Doubts

The British Chiefs of Staff (under the leadership of [prime minister] Winston Churchill) accepted the cross-Channel strategy and the reasoning behind it, but they hedged their acceptance with reservations on scale and timing which betrayed basic doubts whether the Allies were really capable of carrying it off. There is nothing to show that these doubts were not the result of a perfectly sincere and rational military appraisal of the relative strength of the Allies and the Germans. . . . British doubts, especially when accompanied by persistent pleading for immediate action in the Mediterranean, did not strike American crusaders as rational. . . .

The Mediterranean-versus-Northwest-Europe debate, in short, generated a considerable emotional heat which tended to polarize both sides. . . .

The British Military Argument

In the search for the objective fact one should at least start with analysis of what the British *said* were their motives for wanting attacks on North Africa, Sicily, and Italy. In what they said there is not a whisper of politics; they presented a consistent, logical, military argument. In brief, they held that although an attack on northwest Europe must be the ultimate goal of Anglo-American strategy, the German army entrenched in Fortress Europe was a formidable foe—too formidable to be attacked frontally during 1942 and 1943. While preparing for an eventual blow across the Channel, they felt, the Allies must do everything possible to weaken the enemy by accelerating air attacks and by peripheral ground operations in the Mediterranean. Only in this way could the risks of the ultimate cross-Channel attack be reduced to a reasonable gamble. They reiterated their intention of entering Europe not from the south but from the northwest; they always envisaged the final battles as taking place in France and western Germany. They never suggested that a Mediterranean operation should substitute for the cross-Channel invasion.

> [The British] never suggested that a Mediterranean operation should substitute for the cross-Channel invasion.

The military justification for attacking the European underbelly was to stretch the German army and air forces to exhaustion. Attrition of the enemy in the

Mediterranean, together with the air offensive from the west, it was hoped, would relieve some of the pressure on the Soviet Union, enable [Soviet leader Joseph] Stalin's armies to stay in the fight while the Western Allies got ready for the cross-Channel attack, and at the same time weaken the German forces defending France. We now know from German records that the policy of stretch worked, that Allied attacks in the Mediterranean did have the effect of increasing Germany's military responsibilities while reducing her means. . . .

The British Experience

The sincerity of the British military argument should be assessed in the light of their situation during World War II and their previous experience. British memories of the slaughter at Passchendaele and Vimy Ridge in World War I were vivid and bitter. The Prime Minister in particular dreaded a repetition of the bloody trench warfare of 1914–18, which decimated an entire generation. . . . It would have been extraordinary if he had not sought to profit in this war from what he saw to be the clear lesson of the past.

The lesson of experience was reinforced by the disaster of Dunkirk [France]. It should not be forgotten that the British in 1942–43 mustered in their home islands an offensive army of twenty to twenty-five divisions, at a time when the Germans were fighting the Russians with about 225 divisions. On the basis of this contrast alone it was inevitable that Churchill and his Chiefs of Staff should view with misgiving the American plan to deliver a power blow across the Channel. Incidentally, misgiving was more justified at the time than it seems now, looking back at the smashing success achieved by the 1944 invasion. That

> "The truth has always been simple and relatively obvious as long as the strategy debate was separated from its emotional overtones and left in the context of 1942.

success was won by the skill and courage of the Allies, but we now know that it was won against an enemy far weaker than we supposed him to be in 1944. We considerably underestimated the extent to which three years of fighting in Russia and three years of pounding from the air had shattered the German military machine. The fact is that the German armed forces in the West in 1944 were something like the enfeebled and over-extended foe which the British hoped their strategy would produce....

Putting the Strategy Debate in Perspective

The truth has always been simple and relatively obvious as long as the strategy debate was separated from its emotional overtones and left in the context of 1942....

It is hard now to remember a world in which international politics were not dominated by the menace of Communism. It is perhaps harder still to conceive a world in which the immediate hostility of Italy seemed of more moment than the potential hostility of the Soviet Union. But hindsight leads us astray.

Even had the Allied leaders in 1942–43 foreseen the problems of 1950, they would still have had to consider that the paramount job in Europe was to defeat Germany and Italy. They could not plausibly have taken that defeat for granted and so have concerned themselves only with establishing their post-war position vis-à-vis Russia. Defeat of the Axis seems easy now; it did not seem easy then. We tend to think now that that defeat was a foregone conclusion, that it was largely of our making (ours and the British), and that we had only to choose the method that would leave us in the strongest bargaining position afterward. None of these assumptions is true. The war had to be won. It had to be won by supporting Russia whether we liked it or not. It had to be won with the means at hand, and strategy had to be considered a question of fitting the means to the end.

The Need to Keep Russia in the War

In 1942 the main problem confronting Anglo-American strategists was what could be done to help keep Russia in the war. It was realized that without the Red armies, Great Britain and America would be condemned to a long and perhaps inconclusive struggle. With this as the problem, and with the pitifully small resources then available to the Western powers, our choice of action was sharply limited. We decided to invade North Africa because it was necessary to do something at once either to draw German forces away from Russia or to put ourselves in a better defensive position in case Russia were defeated. Nothing more profitable than the North African venture seemed militarily feasible. Once Allied forces were committed in the Mediterranean area, it made irresistible military sense to continue to use them, again on the most fruitful attacks possible within our capabilities. Ships were scarce. German submarines were unchecked in the Atlantic. The shipping requirements to move troops from North Africa to England were almost as large as those to move equivalent troops from the United States to England. To abandon operations in the Mediterranean while building our forces in the United Kingdom meant to relinquish pressure on the enemy in the only place where we could exert it. That is how the Mediterranean strategy developed.

A Balkan invasion was talked about as early as January 1942, but in very general terms. It came under discussion from time to time thereafter but never seriously or at length. . . . The feasibility of a large-scale Balkan invasion seems never to have been debated; no staff work of any consequence was ever done on it. The largest military operation seriously considered was the

> The experience of the past war, on closer study of the facts, does not reveal that we lost the peace through political naïveté in our basic strategy.

establishment of a beachhead to facilitate the supply of Yugoslav guerrillas. This would have been a local incident, not a culmination of strategy. All Mediterranean operations actually mounted were decided without reference to the Balkans. In the light of these facts, it requires a considerable gloss on the mass of surviving records to treat British advocacy of the Mediterranean strategy as a political policy aimed at forestalling Russian occupation of central Europe.

A Strategy Based on Military Judgment

The experience of the past war, on closer study of the facts, does not reveal that we lost the peace through political naïveté in our basic strategy. Rather it shows that in a global war there is not likely to be enough leeway in time, materials, and manpower to allow broad maneuvering for postwar political advantage. Strategy in a full-scale conflict must be based on the facts as they exist, not as they might become a few years hence, and the limitations of these realities are often severe and compelling. The choice of a main battleground must be governed by calculations of military resources, geography, lines of communications, and estimates of enemy capability. In Europe in World War II, . . . the dictates of these military factors were so rigid that the pursuit of secondary and hypothetical objectives might well have jeopardized the battle. . . .

The primary mission in Europe in World War II was to defeat Germany. The military judgment that to carry this out we had to fight in France, not in the Balkans, could not have been politically challenged at the time. The record is clear that it *was* not.

The Allies Invaded France to Reach Germany Ahead of the Soviets

Alexander Canduci

The author of the following viewpoint from 2010 argues that breaking into German leader Adolf Hitler's "Fortress Europe" and bringing a quick end to the war was only a secondary objective of the Normandy landings. He states that the primary objective was to keep the Soviet Union from gaining entry into Europe. In 1944 the United States and Britain already had a second front—in Italy—and were well on their way to defeating Germany. However, they needed the Soviet Union to help win the war but did not trust Soviet leader Joseph Stalin. They were afraid that if they did not open a front in France, the Soviets would overrun not only Germany but much of

SOURCE. Alexander Canduci, "The Fiction that Justified D-Day," *The Greatest Lies in History*, Metro Books, 2010, pp. 204–207, 209–211. Copyright © Sterling Publishing. Copyright © 2009 Murdoch Books Pty Limited. All rights reserved. Reproduced by permission.

the rest of Europe as well, resulting in Communist domination of the continent. Alexander Canduci is a historian and author.

Monday June 2, 2004, was the sixtieth anniversary of the Normandy landings—the first phase of the Allied invasion of northwest Europe. Gathered together on a cliff top at the French coastal town of Arromanches-les-Bains were world leaders, . . . all present to commemorate events that took place on that spot so many years before. . . . There were speeches, glasses raised in toasts, and promises made to remember always the great Allied counter-offensive against Germany. . . . The same platitudes are repeated almost every year and, like all good myths, they are uplifting and inspirational. That is not to denigrate the sacrifices and the lives lost during the Normandy landings, but history tells a different tale, one that questions the need for the Normandy landings and asks why so many brave young men had to lose their lives on those beaches so long ago.

The stated goal of the Normandy landings was to breach [German leader Adolf] Hitler's "Fortress Europe," and to bring an end to the war. While this was certainly a goal, it was not the main point of the operation. Its principal purpose was really to prevent the entry into Europe of an enemy America and Britain feared even more than Hitler—the Soviet Union. The second front was opened in order to stop Soviet troops from overrunning Germany and gaining access to its scientists and the advanced technology they had been busy developing. The real success of the Normandy landings, and the operations that followed, was in preventing the Soviet Union—and the "scourge" of communism—from dominating Europe.

> " The second front was opened in order to stop Soviet troops from overrunning Germany and gaining access to its scientists and . . . advanced technology. "

The Official Story: A Second Front

[Soviet leader Joseph] Stalin was desperate, paranoid, and deeply afraid. His desperation stemmed from the fact that his armies had been driven back with horrendous casualties, leaving the Soviet Union's extensive oilfields exposed to the German onslaught. His paranoia focused on his belief that the Allies had abandoned him to face Hitler's war machine alone while they regrouped. . . . As December 1941 approached, what Stalin really wanted for Christmas was a second front opened against Germany somewhere in Europe. He had to wait until 1942, however, for Allied leaders to feel that the time was right to commit to such a move, in principle at least.

By that stage, a second front was considered vital. . . . Accordingly, [US president Franklin D.] Roosevelt, [British prime minister Winston] Churchill, and Stalin issued a joint statement announcing that a second front was urgently needed. But, at the same time, Churchill informed Soviet Foreign Minister [Vyacheslav Mikhailovich] Molotov that the Allies lacked the resources to undertake an invasion. . . .

From Operation Roundup to Operation Overlord

While the British preferred to attack Germany from the south via Italy—seen as Europe's weak underbelly—the Americans were strongly in favor of an attack via the shortest route, using Britain as a base. The preliminary proposal for a full-scale invasion was named Operation Roundup, which foresaw an invasion in 1943. It was this proposal that formed the basis of the plan that eventually became Operation Overlord, which was delayed until June 1944.

The formal process for organising the invasion did not really get underway until after the Tehran Conference, held in late 1943 between Stalin, Churchill, and Roosevelt. It was there that Roosevelt offered Stalin the

US and Soviet airmen prepare a joint message to the Nazi enemy at an airbase in Russia. **(AFP/Getty Images.)**

guarantee he had been waiting for since June 1941. This was that the Americans and the British would open a second front in France in May 1944, designed to coincide with an escalation of Soviet attacks on Germany's eastern border. Responsibility for the operation was handed to the Supreme Headquarters Allied Expeditionary Force, commanded by General Dwight D. Eisenhower. General Sir Bernard Montgomery was named as commander of the invasion's ground forces, and he was asked to come up with the invasion plan. . . .

The Normandy coast was selected as the preferred landing site. . . . It was argued that landing on a broad front in Normandy would see the Allies ideally positioned for a thrust towards Paris and onwards to the German border. The Normandy coast was also poorly defended, since the Germans did not believe that an invasion would come at that point. . . .

To ensure that Operation Overlord would have the greatest possible chance of success, a series of phoney invasion plans were leaked to the Germans in the weeks leading up to the campaign. They included proposed attacks on the Pas de Calais, the Balkans, the south of France and, most brazen of all, "Operation Fortitude North," which purported to be an invasion plan of Norway. With preparations complete, a force of 156,000 British, Canadian and American troops crossed the English Channel on June 6, 1944, to land on the Normandy beaches and fight their way into history.

> By June 1944 the Allies already had a second front—in Italy.

The Second Front in Italy

The official reason given for launching the landings in Normandy was that this would open a second front in Europe to take the pressure off Soviet troops fighting on the Eastern Front. It was vital for the Western Allies to break into Hitler's "Fortress Europe" in order to bring about a rapid end to the war. This explanation looks superficially plausible, but it ignores the fact that by June 1944 the Allies already had a second front—in Italy. . . .

The second front was accordingly opened in July 1943, when Allied troops landed in Sicily. They spent the next twelve months crossing to the Italian mainland and fighting their way northwards in what proved to be a grueling campaign. When the Italians surrendered in September 1943, the Allies were confident that they could push through Italy very rapidly. But the Germans would have no talk of surrender. . . . German troops put up stiff resistance, slowing the Allied advance significantly. Although Rome didn't fall to the Allies until June 1944, they were nevertheless making steady headway and seemed certain to be able to fight their way into Austria, France, and Germany. In essence, therefore, the Allies were already in Europe. The Western Front had been created and vital German resources were being drained from the Eastern Front. Why, then, should the Allies invade Normandy? The answer was the West's bogeyman—the Soviet Union.

The Real Objective of the Normandy Landings

The Germans were losing the war. It was obvious to everyone by the end of 1943 that the Russians were going to overrun the overstretched German troops on the Eastern Front. Even without the Normandy landings, Germany would therefore have been defeated in late 1945, or possibly early 1946. However, the thought of the Soviets reaching Germany and seizing all its scientists filled Western leaders with horror. Suspecting—rightly as it turned out—that the Soviet Union would turn into an enemy after the fall of the Nazis, Western leaders decided that their troops needed to get to Germany first. But what could they do, with the Italian campaign proceeding so slowly? The answer was an invasion designed to land a sufficient force in northern Europe so that they could get to Germany before Soviet troops had a chance to seize it all for themselves—the Normandy invasion.

> The real objective of the Normandy landings could not be disclosed, since that would have alienated Stalin.

The real objective of the Normandy landings could not be disclosed, since that would have alienated Stalin. The operation was therefore described as the great Western offensive to topple Hitler. While this was certainly a secondary reason for the invasion, the primary reason was always to halt the Soviet advance, which had the potential to go far beyond Germany. There was the possibility that Belgium, France, Greece, and Italy might all be brought under Soviet control if communist troops were allowed to proceed unchecked. Such an outcome was unthinkable. . . .

Churchill's Perspective

Churchill was a vehement anti-Bolshevik [anti-Communist], and nothing had changed his view of Stalin as an enemy to be feared and watched, however useful he might be in the fight against Hitler.

In spite of his wariness of the Soviet Union, Churchill discussed the possibility of opening a second front against the Germans with Stalin as early as 1941. Both men knew that a second front was urgently needed to confront the victorious German military machine and to put pressure on Hitler. However, Churchill was always opposed to a second front in France, preferring to persevere with his plan to attack Italy. He secretly hoped that Germany and the Soviet Union would exhaust each other on the Eastern Front, leaving the Western powers free to deal with both of them easily when the time came. At the Tehran Conference in November 1943, Churchill, Stalin, and Roosevelt discussed Operation Overlord in detail, and agreed that an invasion of France should be launched in May 1944, even though it was already apparent that the war was no longer going smoothly for the Germans. In fact, within a few months it was evident that the Germans had over-reached themselves. While the Allies were making slow progress through Italy, the Russians had not only halted the German advance, but were pushing them back. Defeat for Germany seemed only a matter of time. . . .

Manipulating Stalin

Yet it would seem that Stalin, at Tehran, could not yet see that the Germans were beginning to falter, and was accordingly desperate for another front to be opened in

Europe. He did not predict—as the other Allies did—that the Germans would rapidly become overstretched and that Soviet forces would either hold them indefinitely or eventually overrun them. It was therefore in Stalin's interest to have another front opened in France. The Western Allies, particularly Roosevelt, were also eager for a new front in France, but for different reasons, and they did not want to appear to be too eager in case they aroused Stalin's suspicions about the true objective of Operation Overlord—which was to get to Germany before the Russians did. . . .

> [Stalin] failed to see the real objective of the Normandy invasion and failed to anticipate that America would become the dominant Western power after the war.

Roosevelt appeared to support Stalin, engaging his trust by expressing a desire to see the British Empire brought to heel in the aftermath of war. As American historian Robert Dallek writes: "Roosevelt's candor was calculated to encourage Stalin to see the President as a trustworthy ally. He 'ostentatiously' took Stalin's side in some of his disputes with Churchill." . . . This appearance of disunity worked brilliantly, fitting perfectly with Stalin's view that the British were a major enemy and the principal force to be reckoned with. He failed to see the real objective of the Normandy invasion and failed to anticipate that America would become the dominant Western power after the war. The apparent disunity between Roosevelt and Churchill convinced him instead that there was no great Western conspiracy to oppose the Soviet Union. Instead, he believed that the Western nations were suspicious of each other, and therefore divided. Roosevelt and Churchill manipulated Stalin into believing that it was he who convinced them to launch the Western offensive, and that it was his "alliance" with Roosevelt against Churchill that would ensure the outcome he wanted. . . .

In the Aftermath

The main legacy of the Normandy deception was that it achieved exactly what it set out to do: it prevented communism from gaining more of a foothold in Europe than it eventually did. But it was a close run thing. . . . Soviet and American troops eventually met at the River Elbe on April 25, 1945, cutting Germany in two. Berlin and eastern Germany were taken under Soviet control, with northwest Germany, Denmark, and Holland entering the American and British spheres of influence. It was this outcome that determined the front line in the coming ideological battles of the Cold War. Had it not been for the successful Normandy landings, the situation could have been much worse, with the Red Army overrunning all of Germany, and possibly occupying France and Italy as well.

In the aftermath of the war, the Soviet Union had to be satisfied with control over the eastern half of Europe.

The British Minister Was Railroaded into D-Day

Max Hastings

The following viewpoint maintains that British prime minister Winston Churchill was not happy with the United States' plans for the Allies to invade France and felt that he had been bullied into agreeing to it. The behind-the-scenes political scheming that led to D-Day left Churchill humiliated. For two years he had stood firm against American demands for the invasion because he thought it premature and extremely risky for the Allies. He went along with the plan only because he thought he could stop the invasion from becoming a reality. Publicly he maintained that Britain was deeply committed to Operation Overlord; privately he continued to doubt the wisdom of the plan and to fear that it would result in a devastating number of casualties. Sir Max Hugh Macdonald

SOURCE. Max Hastings, "How Churchill Was Bullied into D-Day— His Most Triumphant Achievement—by the Americans," *Mail Online*, August 24, 2009. www.dailymail.co.uk. Extracted from *Finest Years: Churchill as Warlord*, published by HarperPress on September 3, 2009. Reprinted by permission of HarperCollins Publishers Ltd. Copyright © 2009 Max Hastings, *Finest Years: Churchill as Warlord*. All rights reserved.

Hastings is a British journalist, editor, military historian, and author of numerous books, including *Overlord: D-Day and the Battle for Normandy, 1944*.

The spring of 1944 found [British prime minister Winston] Churchill, in public at least, in [a] typically rousing mood. 'The Germans will suffer very heavy casualties when our band of brothers gets among them,' he wrote to United States President Franklin Roosevelt, quoting Shakespeare's Henry V.

He was referring to their quickly advancing plans for Operation Overlord, the long-awaited Allied assault on the beaches of enemy-occupied France.

But, privately, he was deeply unhappy about the entire project and not best pleased that, as he saw it, he was being railroaded into it by the Americans.

US Pressure, Churchill's Resistance

Ever since the U.S. entered the war, he had been under pressure to invade France, to launch the much-vaunted Second Front and ease the pressure on the Soviet forces fighting [German leader Adolf] Hitler on the other side of Europe.

The Americans seemed oblivious to the scale of the task, and, to the man in the street there, it looked as if the British and their 'fat-headed PM [prime minister]'—as one New Yorker put it—were plain yellow, ducking the fight. . . .

One of Churchill's great achievements was to resist for two years the demands for what he rightly considered would be a premature—and catastrophic—assault on the continental mainland, fiercely contested and possibly ending in a humiliating bloodbath.

His task was made harder by the clamour from the British public for him to act. Even his friends turned on him.

The Indomitable Sir Winston

Sir Winston Churchill has become one of the legends of the twentieth century. A major and then an outstanding political figure in British and world history between 1905 and 1965, he was also a writer of substantial reputation and enormous output. A bibliographer, Frederick Woods, estimated in 1963 that "the total sales of his books in the English language alone are in the region of four million." In speech and written prose he has been noted as a master of the memorable phrase—"blood, toil, tears and sweat" caught the imagination of a generation. Although interest in his essays has been immeasurably enhanced by Churchill's status as statesman and historical writer, they have merit in their own right. . . .

He was evidently the man for a crisis situation, and when it became necessary to reorganize the government in 1940 Churchill succeeded almost by default to the position of prime minister. In the midst of military victory Churchill lost the prime ministry when the Conservatives were defeated in the election of 1945, but he regained the office in 1951. He was knighted by Queen Elizabeth on 24 April 1953. Plagued by the infirmities of age . . . he resigned as prime minister in 1955. . . . He died on 24 January 1965.

SOURCE. *"Winston Churchill, Sir."* Concise Dictionary of British Literary Biography, Vol. 5. *Detroit: Gale Research, 1991.*

Despite being one of Churchill's closest cronies and a former minister in his government, the maverick press baron Lord Beaverbrook launched a 'Second Front Now!' campaign in his newspapers.

A Superior Strategy

Churchill deflected U.S. pressure by persuading Roosevelt—over the heads of the U.S. generals—that the best way to start the fight-back against the Nazis was with U.S. landings in North Africa.

Then, after throwing the Germans out of North Africa, the joint Allied armies would make their way across the Mediterranean to Sicily and Italy, entering Europe through the back door, as Churchill had always intended.

In this, his strategic judgment proved superior to the Americans. France in 1943 would have been a much harder nut to crack. The British Prime Minister had been proved right—so far.

American Persistence

But the suspicious American generals, while committing their troops to the Mediterranean theatre, had never given up on their preferred strategy of a landing in northern France.

> The special relationship between Britain and America . . . was a partnership beset by disagreements that were as much philosophical as military.

In summit meetings with Roosevelt, Churchill found himself signing up to the idea while believing that in the end he could make sure it never happened.

But the uncomfortable reality was that he was no longer in charge of events. He had been Britain's deliverer back in 1940 and 1941—but by the end of 1943 he was not vital to victory. Much as it galled many Britons, it was America who was now in the driving seat.

An Uneasy Relationship

For all [of] Churchill's vaunting of the special relationship between Britain and America, it was a partnership beset by disagreements that were as much philosophical as military.

The key to understanding it is to strip aside the rhetoric of the two leaders and acknowledge that it rested, as relations between states always do, upon perceptions of national interest.

As for the individual personalities involved, there was some genuine sentiment on Churchill's side, but none on Roosevelt's.

The U.S. President had always viewed himself as the senior partner. He paid scant attention to British claims that for years before the U.S. joined the war Britain had

A US Sherman tank passes through a bombed village in Sicily, Italy. Churchill favored continuing this line of entry into Europe instead of the invasion through Normandy. **(Galerie Bilderwelt/Getty Images.)**

played the nobler part, pouring forth blood and enduring bombardment in a lone struggle for freedom.

He paid only lip service to the collective gratitude owed by the democracies to Britain for single-handedly standing up to Hitler.

The American Perception of the British

Churchill liked to assert that, far from owing a huge cash debt to the U.S. when the war was over, Britain should be recognised as a creditor for its lone defence of freedom in 1940–41. This was never plausible.

Polls showed that most Americans—70 per cent—were implacable in their belief that at the end of the war the British should repay the billions they had received from the U.S. in Lend-Lease supplies. They stuck to the notion that Britain was a wealthy nation. They failed to grasp the extent of her financial exhaustion.

In fact, Roosevelt felt scant sympathy for his transatlantic ally. He had visited Britain several times as a young man, but never revealed much liking for the country.

He perceived hypocrisy in its pretensions as a bastion of democracy and freedom while it sustained a huge empire of subject peoples in Africa and Asia and denied them democratic representation.

Americans were overwhelmingly hostile to Britain for refusing to countenance self-government for India. . . .

He [Churchill] was disgusted by the holier-than-thou attitude of Americans on the matter. He deemed it rank cant for a nation that had itself colonised a continent, dispossessing and largely exterminating its indigenous population, and which still practised racial segregation, to harangue others about the treatment of native peoples.

A Definite Difference of Opinions

But Roosevelt's belief was that the day of empire was done. He co-operated with Churchill's nation in order to defeat Hitler. Thereafter, he proposed to reshape the world in accordance with American concepts of morality.

Despite his acquaintance with foreign parts having been confined to gilded European holidays with his millionaire father, he had a boundless appetite to alter the world. He regarded the future without fear.

Churchill, by contrast, was full of apprehension about the threats a new world posed to Britain's greatness. It was from these two very different perspectives that the Allies continued uneasily to conduct their joint affairs.

For his part, Churchill continued to duck and weave, sustaining the fiction that an Overlord operation in the spring of 1944 was an option rather than an absolute commitment. He pressed for the thrust up through Italy to remain as the Allies' immediate priority.

They should seize the moment in the Mediterranean, he argued to Roosevelt, rather than stake everything on a highly dangerous and speculative cross-Channel attack.

But Churchill was wrong about this. Italy was a difficult battlefield, easy to defend, difficult to advance in. If efforts had been concentrated there, D-Day would have been delayed until 1945.

> "Churchill, by contrast, was full of apprehension about the threats a new world posed to Britain's greatness."

A Time of Challenge for Churchill

It was American resolution alone that ensured the operational timetable for D-Day was maintained, while the Prime Minister expended political capital in a struggle with Washington that he was not only bound to lose, but which he deserved to lose.

The detailed planning for Overlord went on despite him. He was furious when seven British divisions he had wanted to throw into capturing Rome were withdrawn from the line to return to Britain to prepare for D-Day. But there was little he could do to stop it happening. . . .

> The best that can be said is that at operational level, the two nations' armed forces worked adequately together, no more.

Churchill's misgivings persisted. He thought the forces being deployed were insufficiently strong to take on what he knew were the superior fighting qualities of the German army. 'Struck by how very tired and worn out the Prime Minister looks now,' wrote Jock Colville, his private secretary.

He had even lost Roosevelt's ear. His appeals to the President were simply referred to General George Marshall, the U.S. Army chief.

A "Glorious Fiction"

Despite all this, Churchill maintained the idea of 'an absolute brotherhood' in arms with the U.S. But the best that can be said is that at operational level, the two nations' armed forces worked adequately together, no more.

In his speeches between 1940 and 1945, Churchill created a glorious fiction of shared British and American purposes. He never hinted to his own public, still less the transatlantic one, his frustrations and disappointments about Roosevelt and his policies.

As D-Day approached, Churchill's attitude was bewilderingly complex, perhaps even to himself. He thrilled to a historic military operation, the success of which would go far to fulfil every hope he had cherished since 1940.

He emphasised to his own people, as well as to the Americans, that Britain was wholeheartedly committed. He took the keenest interest in every detail of the invasion plans. But he never ceased to lament the realities of the campaign.

An Awareness of the Realities

He knew that the United States, with 60 divisions in the field against Britain's 18, would dominate operations in north-west Europe once the Allies were ashore. The British war effort would attain its apogee [peak] on June 6, 1944. Thereafter, it must shrink before the sad gaze of its helmsman. . . .

But above all, he was nervous of failure. Every rational calculation suggested that the Allies, aided by surprise, air power and massive resources, should get ashore successfully. He nonetheless nursed terrible fears of catastrophic casualties.

> No one knew better than [Churchill] the terrible consequences for the Allies if, for whatever reason, D-Day failed.

No one knew better than he the extraordinary fighting power of Hitler's army, and the limitations of the citizen soldiers of Britain and the U.S. No one knew better than he the terrible consequences for the Allies if, for whatever reason, D-Day failed.

The peoples of Britain and the U.S. would suffer a crippling blow to their morale and confidence in their leaders. And disaster in Normandy might precipitate the end for him. . . .

On the night of June 5, as [Churchill's wife] Clementine Churchill departed for bed, he told her: 'By the time you wake up in the morning, 20,000 young men may have been killed.' . . .

The D-Day Landings

His fears proved unfounded. The D-Day landings represented the greatest feat of military organisation in history, a triumph of planning, logistics and above all human endeavour.

The massed airborne assault on the flanks which began in darkness, the air and naval bombardment followed by the dawn dash up the fire-swept shoreline by more than 100,000 British, American and Canadian engineers, infantrymen, armoured crews and gunners, achieved brilliant success.

The invaders fought doggedly through flame and smoke, wire entanglements, pillboxes, minefields and gun positions to stake out the claims of the Allied armies inside Hitler's Europe.

Churchill followed the progress of the landings hour by hour in his map room in the Cabinet bunker under Whitehall. To few men in the world did the battle mean so much.

Instead of the carnage he feared, just 3,000 American, British and Canadian troops died on D-Day. By nightfall, in places the invaders had advanced several miles inland.

A long and terrible struggle lay ahead, as invaders and defenders raced to reinforce their rival armies in Normandy. There were days to come when more Allied soldiers perished than on June 6. But the triumph of Overlord was assured.

A Protagonist in WWII History

On June 12, Churchill was at last allowed to visit the invasion beachhead in Normandy himself, an expedition he relished. He was enchanted by the spectacle of the invasion coast, cabling to the Soviet leader Stalin: 'It is a wonderful sight to see this city of ships stretching along the coast for nearly 50 miles.' . . .

After D-Day, but for the Prime Minister's personal contribution, Britain would have become a backwater, a supply centre and aircraft carrier for the American-led armies in Europe.

In 1944–45 Churchill exercised much less influence upon events than in 1940–43. But without him, his country would have seemed a mere exhausted victim of the conflict, rather than the protagonist which he was determined that Britain should be seen to remain until the end.

Stalin Did Not Really Want a Second Front in 1944

Murray Sager

The following viewpoint, written in 2009, contemplates Soviet leader Joseph Stalin's motives for continuing to call for the Allies to open a second front in Europe. The call made sense right after the Germans invaded the Soviet Union. It ceased to do so in late 1943 after the Soviets destroyed the German 6th Army in the Battle of Stalingrad. Early on Stalin considered the call to be in the Soviets' best interest. A second front would enable the Soviets to get a toehold in and spread communism throughout Europe. According to the author, continuing to call for a second front even when it was not logical would keep the Western Allies in line. It also would keep the Allies supplying the Soviets and continuing a heavy bombing offensive. Murray Sager is a writer who has contributed numerous articles to magazines.

SOURCE. Murray Sager, "The Second Front: by the Time the Allies Landed in Normandy in June 1944, the Soviet Union Was Already on the Way to Defeating Hitler's Nazis on Its Own," *Esprit de Corps*, January 1, 2009. Copyright © S.R. Taylor Publishing. All rights reserved. Reproduced by permission.

The *Globe and Mail* [Canada's national newspaper] has been running the series "Dear Sweetheart," the letters of a Canadian soldier training in England written to his wife in Canada. There's not much action in them. There are stories of courts martial, moves from one camp to another, social life, dances and food, but no actual fighting. This was typical for most Canadian soldiers in England. They were there long before the Americans arrived, and waited, endlessly training, but rarely fighting. They must have wondered what they were doing there, and when the action might commence; [Soviet leader Joseph] Stalin wondered too.

Reactions to the Call for a Second Front

The call to open a second front was a regular event during the last war. Initiated by Stalin and echoed by the western allies, the second front was deemed to be necessary for the relief of the Soviets and a successful conclusion to the war. It was a logical call, at least until the Germans were defeated at Stalingrad. Russia was under the most severe pressure, coming very close to losing Moscow and perhaps the war, so any distraction the west could provide was both welcome and common sense. The call for a second front struck a chord with workers in Great Britain and to a lesser extent the United States.

The America leaders were keen on the idea as well, perhaps less cautious than the British (at this stage at least) in their dealings with Stalin, and also confident of their ability to invade the continent soon after becoming fully involved in the war. The British were fearful of the potential casualties from an invasion of the continent, and increasingly aware of both their financial bankruptcy and decreasing influence on the allies' strategies. British caution about Stalin's intentions also led them to advocate other approaches to fighting the war, keeping an eye on their interests east of Suez [Egypt], and hoping

Photo on following page: Russian leader Joseph Stalin greets the public in Moscow in 1941. **(AP Photo.)**

PERSPECTIVES ON MODERN WORLD HISTORY

to prevent a Soviet presence on the eastern Mediterranean. Hence, while the US was pushing for an invasion of France in 1943, the British succeeded in convincing the Americans to pursue a Mediterranean approach.

"Second Fronts" Opened in the West

In the meantime, one or even two "second fronts" were opened in the west, the now often maligned bombing offensive, and lend lease in its Soviet version which included the Maskan highway and the airbases associated with it, the Arctic convoys to Murmansk and the road link through Persia. These supplied food, aircraft, trucks, radio equipment and clothing in vast quantities. The bombing offensive clearly resulted in a withholding of men and materiel from the German efforts on the eastern front, as well as restricting the growth of German industry. But Stalin apparently wanted more, specifically an early invasion of France.

> Stalin apparently wanted more, specifically an early invasion of France.

There have been claims that the Dieppe raid [in France] in August 1942 was a response to Stalin's demands. Earlier that year at the second Washington conference, the British and Americans had agreed to launch a second front that year. [US president Franklin D.] Roosevelt even made a commitment of 120,000 troops to [Soviet foreign minister Vyacheslav Mikhailovich] Molotov. In addition to attempting to satisfy Stalin, the British especially were in need of morale boosting. Tobruk [Libya] had fallen to [German general Erwin] Rommel in June 1942, unacceptable shipping losses had meant a temporary stop to convoys in the Atlantic and German armies were in sight of Moscow. The Canadian army in Britain needed a boost as well. Lack of action was resulting in increasing unrest among the troops, low morale and poor "optics." Other colonial forces were in action, why weren't the Canadians? So Dieppe might have been an answer to all these issues.

But Dieppe was a failure. Had it been a success, it would still not have constituted a second front in the west. There were no plans to do anything more than examine a radar site, test defences and bring home prisoners. There were insufficient resources and no plan to break out of Dieppe if that became possible. Dieppe was no more than a raid in force, designed to achieve similar results to the [British] raid on St. Nazaire [France], and it certainly wouldn't have convinced Stalin of the west's good intentions, even if it had been a success.

Stalin's Logic

But did Stalin really want a second front? His calls for an invasion of France were logical during the time between the invasion of the Soviet Union and at least until late 1943 and the defeat of the 6th Army at Stalingrad. The outcome of the war must have been clear to him at that point. There was no doubt a long and bloody slogging match to be fought, with setbacks as well as more victories to come, but of the conclusion, there was no question. Stalin's thoughts about what that victory might look like included, or were perhaps dominated by the question of how far he would be able to physically impose Soviet influence in Europe. He was

> At about this point, calling for a second front would surely have struck him as out of date and undesirable.

after all, schooled in the theory of the collapse of the European capitalist system as an inevitable result of its inherent contradictions. This war was a vindication of this theory, which would allow the revolution to spread, as envisaged by [Russian revolutionary Vladimir] Lenin, throughout Europe.

At about this point, calling for a second front would surely have struck him as out of date and undesirable. He continued to do so though, managing to raise the fear in western leaders' minds that without a second front, he might be tempted to come to a second non-aggression pact with [German leader Adolf] Hitler. And so the Americans finally insisted on an invasion in the summer of 1944. The British were still dragging their heels. By now the pattern was set. The propaganda machine roused the western workers to support their glorious Soviet allies, and lend-lease supplies continued to flow east.

Ideally this should have satisfied Stalin. He was getting the goods without the problems of having to negotiate with the west or even have them on the continent. It must have been a much more attractive idea to let the west dither about in the Med[iterranean] and plod their slow way north through Italy, than to have them also racing towards Berlin. How much more attractive to contemplate a free hand Europe, first crushing the Germans in Germany and then continuing with a series of mopping-up operations, stopping finally on the Bay of Biscay, or even facing Gibraltar.

Bad Scenarios for Stalin

What would really have worried him would have been a combined and committed attack by the west through the Balkans and then up into Czechoslovakia. There was no danger of this. The Americans were convinced British plans were mainly centred on securing and maintaining India, which the Americans were opposed to on principle. The Americans, especially Roosevelt, were at this time trusting of Uncle Joe [Stalin] and his democratic intentions in Eastern Europe. The worst possible scenario for the Soviets . . . was the liberation of buffer states before the final collapse of Germany.

Almost as bad for Stalin would have been a successful invasion of France in the summer of 1943: the American intention. Had the bombing offensive been re-directed to tactical targets, and the entire western allied armies been brought to bear on northern France, rather than Italy, this could have been successful and would have hit the Germans at a very low point in their morale. Stalingrad had just been lost and the bombing offensive had not yet reached the point where it actually strengthened German resolve. What then for Stalin, with the Battle of Kursk to come, German armies still deep in Soviet territory and the west heading for Berlin and likely to reach it long before him? Such an outcome would have made the Soviet war nothing more than sacrifice, without even the satisfaction of destroying the Germans on their own turf. Leningrad, Stalingrad, scorched earth would all have been for nothing. The sacrifices demanded of the Russian population, and willingly given beyond the sacrifices demanded of any other population, would have gone unrewarded and the consequences of that level of dissatisfaction could have overthrown even Stalin. Additionally he would then have been faced with some version of a united Germany entirely within the influence of the west, and probably the buffer states between Russia and Germany also within the west and starting on a path of developing truly democratic governments.

Why Stalin Called for a Second Front

So why the call for a second front? One conclusion must simply be that Stalin was exercising his known realism. There was probably little chance of a second front before 1944 and he knew it, but making the call kept the west on its toes, kept the supplies coming, ensured that the bombing war was conducted to its maximum extent. Stalin was perfectly capable of making the most sudden and unexpected moves. However unlikely another pact with Hitler might have been, the awareness of Stalin's track record made this a central fear, far after it logically should have been. On the morning of June 6, 1944, Stalin must have been wishing for yet another postponement.

D-Day Was Predominantly a British Operation

Ken Ford

A historian argues in the following viewpoint from 2009 that Britain's role in D-Day has been minimized and greatly underrated thanks to Hollywood's Americanization of the event. He asserts that many young people who see American movies and television shows about D-Day are unaware of the truth: that D-Day was largely a British operation. D-Day planning, for example, was begun by the office of the chief of staff to the Supreme Allied Commander in London. Also, most of the ships that carried the invasion force on D-Day belonged to the British Royal Navy and Merchant Marine, and three of the five landing beaches targeted for the invasion were allocated to the British Second Army. Ken Ford is a British military historian and the author of more than twenty books on World War II, including *Caen 1944: Montgomery's Break-Out Attempt* and *Overlord: The D-Day Landings*.

SOURCE. Ken Ford, "So Sorry Monsieur Sarkozy, D-Day Was a Very BRITISH Triumph," *Mail Online*, June 9, 2009. http://dailymail .co.uk. Copyright © Ken Ford/Osprey Publishing. All rights reserved. Reproduced by permission.

enry Ford famously said history is bunk.

And anyone who watched [French president] Nicolas Sarkozy exploit the D-Day commemorations for a cynical photo-opportunity with [US president] Barack Obama could be forgiven for believing the French president, at the very least, suffers from politically expedient amnesia.

In a blatant attempt to cosy up to America's new President, Mr Sarkozy seemed keen to reduce D-Day to a Hollywood-friendly French and American effort to rid Europe of the evil Nazis.

The only surviving head of state who actually served in the conflict, the Queen [of England], was not deemed worthy to be invited to the celebrations, further marginalising Britain's efforts.

There is no doubt that Hollywood blockbusters such as *Saving Private Ryan* and the TV mini-series *Band of Brothers* are responsible for an unmistakable—and untruthful—Americanisation of the Normandy landings.

A Need to Remember the British Contribution

But there is really no excuse for Mr Sarkozy to forget that the liberation of his country was only possible because of Britain's contribution to the war.

In truth, the Parisian political elite has never quite forgiven the old enemy for liberating it from the Germans.

Its own collaborationist past has always been an embarrassment to whatever government is in power, for it reminds them that its army, then the largest in the world, capitulated while Britain fought on alone against [German leader Adolf] Hitler.

This nationalistic attitude is in stark contrast with that of the French people themselves, who remember and appreciate the sacrifice British Tommies [soldiers] made.

> " The truth is that D-Day was predominantly a British operation. "

Visit any of the towns liberated by the British and Canadians and you will find a wealth of memorials and celebrations to mark their freedom, along with great numbers of the local population who turn out to welcome any veteran who visits.

British Contributions to D-Day Planning

The truth is that D-Day was predominantly a British operation.

The planning for this great enterprise was begun by the office of the Chief of Staff to the Supreme Allied Commander (COSSAC) in London.

The head of COSSAC was Lieutenant-General Frederick Morgan, a British officer who had served in France in 1940. It was Morgan who was given the task of planning for the invasion of North-West Europe.

Most of the aerial reconnaissance work related to the plan was carried out by the RAF [Royal Air Force], as was the job of recording and plotting German fortifications and beach obstacles.

Intelligence about enemy troops and their coastal defences gathered by the French underground was organised, processed and supported by the men and women of the British Special Operations Executive in London.

Brave individuals from the Combined Operations Pilotage Parties visited shorelines on the other side of the Channel stealthily by night, carrying out beach reconnaissance.

These silent commandos gathered data on currents, tides and samples of sand and gravel from all the beaches, not just in Normandy but along the whole length of the coastline of North-West Europe.

When the invasion actually took place, the Navy and the military knew, thanks to British efforts, exactly what to expect on the far shore.

Photo on following page: British troops watch the plume of water as a depth charge they dropped on a suspected German U-boat position explodes off the coast of Caen, France, in Normandy on June 7, 1944. (Mansell/Time & Life Pictures/Getty Images.)

British Contributions on D-Day

The D-Day armada which carried the invasion force was largely made up of ships of the Royal Navy and the British Merchant Marine.

The bomber forces that pounded strategic targets inside France were a combined effort by the USAAF and the RAF. The British organised a ground support air command especially to support troops in battle.

This RAF 2nd Tactical Air Force flew low-level missions against individual road, rail and military targets all over northern France, interfering with enemy troop movements and supply columns before the invasion.

In the Channel, Royal Navy vessels continually attacked German shipping movements and swept the seas of enemy craft.

On D-Day itself three of the five landing beaches (Sword, Juno and Gold) were allocated to [the] British Second Army, which included the Canadian 3rd Division. The other two beaches (Omaha and Utah) were American.

On June 6, 1944, ten Allied divisions landed in France: five American, four British and one Canadian.

> The British and Canadian formations were much larger than the Americans.

The British and Canadian formations were much larger than the Americans for they had extra troops and armoured units attached to them—the basic U.S. division contained around 11,000 men, the British numbers were about 18,000.

Eisenhower Was Not the First Choice for Commander

The Supreme Commander for the invasion of Europe was an American, General Dwight D. Eisenhower, but he was not the first choice of either nation.

Britain favoured its most senior officer, the Chief of the Imperial General Staff, Field Marshal Sir Alan

Brooke, for the task and [US president Franklin D.] Roosevelt wanted America's top general, the U.S. Chief of Staff, General George Marshall, as Supreme Commander.

President Roosevelt and Prime Minister Winston Churchill eventually decided, perhaps diplomatically after careful consideration, that these two leading soldiers were probably too valuable in their present positions to be spared, and so the job went to Eisenhower.

In recognition of the great role that Britain was to play, it was also decided that Eisenhower's deputy, Air Chief Marshal Sir Arthur Tedder, and all the other senior subordinate commanders, would be British.

Thus General Sir Bernard Montgomery commanded [the] 21st Army Group, which included all army troops both British and American that landed on D-Day; Admiral Sir Bertram Ramsay presided over the Royal Navy and U.S. Navy as head of the Allied Naval Expeditionary Force, and the USAAF and the RAF contingent was led by Air Chief Marshal Sir Trafford Leigh-Mallory.

I wonder if President Sarkozy and the Americans remember all this? I also wonder if our own children understand Britain's role in the invasion?

The Enigma Code Machine: The True Story

A recent study in schools showed a decline in the number of pupils sitting the history GCSE [General Certificate of Secondary Education]. Many young people now learn about our past through the prism of Hollywood.

Britain was shocked when a recent war film U-571 showed that the first German naval Enigma code machine was captured by the Americans from a German submarine.

The machine was in fact captured by men from HMS Bulldog in May 1941 before the U.S. had even entered the war.

There were 15 subsequent captures of Enigma machines during the war, only one made by Americans.

That feat was made later on in the struggle when the German naval codes had already been well and truly cracked by British code-breakers at Bletchley Park [estate in England].

Another Hollywood Distortion of History

The latest affront to history comes from Quentin Tarantino's war film *Inglourious Basterds*, (yes that is the way he spells the title), starring Brad Pitt.

It shows an American-led group of Jewish soldiers working behind enemy lines. They delight in assassinating Germans and sickening atrocities, including the gathering of German scalps.

In fact, there was a unit of Jewish commandos, No. 3 (Jewish) Group. It was part of British No. 10 Commando.

The men in the unit served with great distinction, not as blood-crazy scalp-hunters, but as brave and honourable professional soldiers.

A German friend of mine once told me that it is the victors who write the history of the war.

It seems now that the role is increasingly being taken over by film-makers in Hollywood—aided and abetted by Nicolas Sarkozy.

Americans Played the Major Role in the Breakout Battle of Normandy

Christopher Bellamy

In the following viewpoint, the author maintains that although the British and Canadians contributed to the breakout from the Normandy beachhead, US troops played the most significant role in the battle. He writes that the Americans demonstrated impres sive mobility by advancing first south and then east towards Paris, while the British remained mired in attempts to take the city of Caen from the Germans. The Americans demonstrated great flexibility and ingenuity by improvising a device that made it possible for them to get through hedgerows that served as barriers. They reacted extremely quickly to British general Bernard Montgomery's change in original plans for the Allies and adapted with astonishing speed following initial setbacks. Christopher Bellamy is an author and has served as a professor of military science and doctrine and as director of the Security Studies Institute, Cranfield University, United Kingdom.

For all the battle experience of [British general Bernard] Montgomery's veterans from the fighting in North Africa, and the flying start the successful landings [in Normandy] had given them, it was the Americans who were to play the more prominent and decisive role in the break-out battle, and after initial setbacks, they adapted with extraordinary speed—as [British prime minister Winston] Churchill later commented.

> The Americans were able to develop a natural flair for a war of manoeuvre.

The British got locked in a slugging match for [the French city of] Caen, while the more mobile American forces pushed south and then swung east towards Paris. Veterans of the desert war [in Africa] found the close, broken country, riddled with ditches and thick hedgerows, claustrophic and intimidating, while the Americans were able to develop a natural flair for a war of manoeuvre. Historians still disagree whether that was the original plan or just the way the battle developed.

Montgomery's Way of Thinking

The British commander of the invasion ground forces, General Bernard Montgomery . . . was severely criticised for not taking a more aggressive role. Montgomery could justly claim to have drawn in strong forces which facilitated the American break-out, but that may not have been his original aim.

It is possible he hoped to fight the mobile battle east of Caen with the British armour from Lt-Gen Miles

Dempsey's Second Army, while the American First Army under Lt-Gen Omar Bradley got on with the mundane business of securing the ports of Cherbourg and Brest. It may have been lucky for the Allies that a different plan was forced on him.

By 10 June [1944], the separate D-Day beachheads had been linked and the Americans were attacking inland towards Cherbourg, while the British were preparing to take Caen. Initially the US forces in the west encountered terrain which was more difficult than that facing the British to the east.

US generals George S. Patton and Omar Bradley (left to right) share a laugh with British general Bernard Law Montgomery while discussing strategy and the progress of the Normandy campaign on July 7, 1944. (Time Life Pictures/US Signal Corps/Getty Images.)

British Failure at Caen

But despite heavy bombardment of Caen and of the German positions to the south, the British attempt to outflank the city at Villers-Bocage, to the west on 10–12 June failed, as did another attempt to the west by 15th Scottish Division from 24 June to 1 July.

A third British and Canadian attempt to capture Caen from 18–20 June, Operation Goodwood, which tried to cut behind it to the east using a strong armoured force, also failed. The US forces, meanwhile, occupied the Cotentin peninsula and forced Cherbourg to surrender on 27 June.

The argument about Montgomery's original plan has raged since the end of the war. Brigadier Kenneth McLean, a senior planner, said that "for Montgomery to say he was holding the Germans so Bradley could break out was absolute rubbish and a complete fabrication that only developed after he was stopped outside Caen."

A Shortage of Ammunition and Troops

Montgomery later said his forces were short of ammunition and troops. He said: "At best it would have been touch and go whether we could take it or not . . . the British Army was a wasting asset. The War Office told me before D-Day that it could guarantee reinforcements only for the first month. It would have been very easy for me to yield to public criticism and American pressure and to have made greater efforts to gain ground on this flank."

Manpower was a constant concern. By early July the British were seriously short of trained infantry, as their casualties had been heavier and those among other units lighter than expected.

It seems that Montgomery was sensible to proceed as he did, maintaining constant pressure on Caen to draw the Germans in while Bradley prepared to attack in the west. But at the end of June the Americans, too, were stuck in the difficult terrain.

American Ingenuity and Success

But the Americans solved the problem with a device improvised from the obstacles the Germans had scattered on the beaches. The steel stakes were sharpened and fitted to the front of hundreds of US tanks, enabling them to gouge their way through the hedgerows. It was an example of the flexibility that characterised the well-equipped US forces.

Little by little the Germans were forced back until on 17 July Bradley's Army was formed up on the line Lessay-Periers-St Lo. On 25 July, the Americans launched Operation Cobra, breaking through west of St Lo.

It was unexpectedly successful because most of the German forces had been drawn east to Caen. Only one Panzer [German armored] division, the Lehr, was in the area to attempt to block the attack. The heavy air bombardment also helped, but not until after one of the worst "friendly fire" incidents of the war, in which planes from the Eighth Air Force dropped bombs short, killing 111 Americans including a general.

Finding resistance weaker than expected, the US forces advanced rapidly. The American Third Army, under Lt-Gen George Patton . . . , turned west towards Brest, to fulfil the plan to capture the port.

A Change of Plan

But on 4 August, Montgomery issued the first change to the original plan. Patton was to swing eastwards in a wide-reaching attack across the rear of the German armies. It may not have been the original scheme, but Montgomery deserves some credit for exploiting success and the particular qualities of Patton and the American forces. The British and the Canadians were to continue attacking southwards towards Caen.

The Germans tried to cut off the advancing Americans by attacking west from [the commune of] Mortain, but the Allies intercepted their coded transmissions and defeated them on 6 August. This had drawn German armour from Caen, which in turn allowed the British and Canadians to push south.

The mobile US forces then swept round the Germans to trap 50,000 of them in the so-called "Falaise pocket" [area between four French cities near Falaise]. The Canadians reached Falaise on 15 August and the US XV Corps had reached Argentan two days earlier.

> As Churchill noticed, the Americans displayed a remarkable ability to adapt.

But despite efforts to seal the pocket, by now only 15 miles wide, the majority of the German forces escaped across the Seine by ferry and temporary bridges. The pocket was finally closed on 20 August, the Allies inflicting fearful destruction with artillery and aircraft, including rocket-armed Typhoon fighter bombers.

Unfair Criticism

Modern US military analysts have criticised the Allies for not attempting a bigger encirclement all the way to the Seine [River]. But Patton stopped his encircling spearheads at Argentan to wait for the slower British and Canadians.

The British official history describes the British left flank as "the pivot on which the main stroke would hinge. It must always remain secure or the whole movement might lose its balance."

That was not the original plan, nor is it correct to view the British and Canadians as locked in a static battle while the Americans did all the manoeuvre. When the Americans drew in German forces, the British and Canadians advanced.

Fighting together in north-west Europe for the first time in the era of mechanised warfare, the British and US forces were each finding their feet. As Churchill noticed, the Americans displayed a remarkable ability to adapt.

Patton, audacious to the core, converted the local breakthrough by the First Army into a theatre-wide break-out that only ground to a halt in September because of fuel shortages.

Leadership Differences Contributed Greatly to the Outcome of D-Day

J. Justin Gustainis

The following viewpoint argues that the Allied victory and the German failure on D-Day were due in great part to the difference in Allied and German leadership. The author writes that the Allies had a true leader in US general Dwight D. Eisenhower, a commander with military training and experience, strong diplomatic and administrative skills, on-target decision-making capabilities, and an unwavering commitment to teamwork. German leadership suffered from professional disagreement between the commanding general and his superior over the scenarios of invasion and from German leader Adolf Hitler's insistence on having final authority and his inclination to make poor, conflict-ridden military decisions.

SOURCE. J. Justin Gustainis, "D-Day," *Encyclopedia of Leadership*, Sage Reference, vol. 1, 2004, pp. 313–316. Encyclopedia of Leadership by Goethals, George R. Copyright © 2004. Reproduced with permission of Sage Publications Inc. in book format and in CD ROM/DVD ROM via Copyright Clearance Center.

J. Justin Gustainis is a professor at Plattsburgh State University of New York and the author of several books as well as numerous scholarly papers, award-winning articles, and book chapters.

The amphibious assault by the Allies on the beaches of Normandy, France, on 6 June 1944—D-Day— was the largest military operation of World War II, perhaps the largest in all of modern warfare. Although the cost in money, materiel, and lives was high, the assault was a success, and it spelled the beginning of the end for Germany's Third Reich.

Overlord Concept, Objectives, and Planning

The assault, code named "Overlord" by the Allies, involved two years of planning and preparation. The basic concept was simple but bold: to defeat Germany in western Europe, where it was strongest, and thus to inflict massive damage on the Nazi war machine and open the way for a thrust into the German heartland. At the same time, a successful invasion would take pressure off the Soviets on the eastern front, allowing the Soviet leader Joseph Stalin to organize an effective counteroffensive against the German invaders there. The Allies had sufficient resources to launch only a single invasion, so Overlord involved the rolling of some large dice. The logistical nightmare aside, invasion planning was complicated by the necessity of integrating a multinational fighting force and command structure, by the problem of overcoming the intricate coastal defenses that the Nazis had constructed everywhere an invasion might be possible, and by the Nazis' certain knowledge that the Allies were coming—even if the Nazis did not know exactly when or where.

The success of the Allies and the failure of the Germans at Normandy hinged on a variety of factors. One of the most important of these—on both sides—was leadership.

The Allied Command

The head of the committee planning Operation Overlord, and also the commander of the invasion itself, was U.S. Gen. Dwight D. Eisenhower. Because the United States was providing the largest component of the invasion force (sixty divisions, compared to the twenty provided by Britain and Canada together), U.S. President Franklin D. Roosevelt and British Prime Minister Winston Churchill had agreed that a U.S. military leader must assume command. Eisenhower, as it turned out, was an inspired choice.

> Eisenhower, as it turned out, was an inspired choice [for commander].

Eisenhower's Background and Experience

A graduate of West Point, Eisenhower had been unable to secure a combat command during World War I and spent the war training armored units in the United States. During the 1930s he served on the staff of Gen. Douglas MacArthur, and as war loomed in the early 1940s he was assigned to Gen. George C. Marshall, Army chief of staff. As early as March 1942 he wrote a memorandum for Marshall that urged that the primary Allied target be Germany and suggested that the surest road to victory lay through western Europe.

Eisenhower commanded "Operation Torch," the British and U.S. assault on North Africa in November 1942. The initial assault was a success, but as Eisenhower's forces moved inland they came up against the German Afrika Corps led by the formidable Gen. Erwin Rommel. In February 1943, Rommel's forces attacked at the Kasserine Pass and inflicted a disastrous defeat on the Allied forces. However, the test of a true leader is not that he makes no mistakes, but rather that he learns from those he does make. Eisenhower was a true leader.

Eisenhower's Diplomatic Skill

Although military culture fosters authoritarian leadership, Eisenhower understood that planning and carrying out Operation Overlord would require more than

General Dwight D. Eisenhower rides in a motorcade through New York's Central Park on August 1, 1945, celebrating the end of World War II eight years before being elected president of the United States. (Keystone/Getty Images.)

simply issuing orders. A task so immense would require cooperation, consensus, and the delegation of a certain amount of responsibility. From the start, Eisenhower's watchword for Overlord was *teamwork*. He was determined that the U.S. and British soldiers work together, despite all the cultural differences and potential rivalries involved. Indeed, Eisenhower's skills as a diplomat were equally as important as his military ability in President Roosevelt's decision to give Eisenhower command of the operation.

Eisenhower had set a system of unified British and U.S. command during Operation Torch, and he employed a similar system (although on a much larger scale) in organizing for Overlord. U.S. and British officers were integrated into a single staff and encouraged to work as a team. He is known to have said, "I don't care if somebody gets called a son of a bitch. That's natural. But I'm damned if he'll be called an *American* son of a bitch, or a *British* son of a bitch." When some U.S. officers complained about their British superiors . . . Eisenhower told them to grin and bear it and to do their jobs.

Eisenhower's Administrative and Decision-Making Skills

Eisenhower was a brilliant administrator. He could be patient when required (which was often), but he would allow himself to lose his famous temper if he thought someone needed shaking up. He emphasized the need for consensus among the planners, but he recognized that the ultimate responsibility was his alone. He could be stubborn when he felt the operation was being endangered. When the Royal Air Force balked at being under his command, Eisenhower told Churchill that either the command would be unified or it would have to look for a new

> Historians agree that Eisenhower's leadership leading up to the D-Day invasion was masterful.

Dwight D. Eisenhower, Supreme Commander

On Christmas Eve of 1943, after operating without a leader for nearly a year, the Allied forces assembling in Britain learned who was to have the momentous task of completing their preparations for the invasion of France and launching the assault. That day in Washington, President [Franklin D.] Roosevelt announced over the radio that the chief of the Supreme Headquarters of the Allied Expeditionary Force (SHAEF) was to be General Dwight D. Eisenhower.

Two years earlier, Eisenhower had been so little known, even in America, that a newspaper had called him "Lt. Col. D.D. Ersenbeing"; now, he was so famous that King George VI of England requested his autograph for a relative. Eisenhower's swift rise—first to commander of the North Africa invasion and then to chief of U.S. troops in the European theater—was due primarily to his ability to weld leaders with assertive personalities and differing national interests into a winning team. That talent had impressed German spies and they noted it in their reports. But some Allied observers considered Eisenhower unqualified for his new job. They pointed out that he had never personally commanded troops in battle and they accused him of being indecisive and overly conciliatory—more an arbitrator than a dynamic leader. Eisenhower's consideration for the British prompted several U.S. officers to grumble, "Ike is the best commander the British have." Alert to the charge, Eisenhower stopped carrying his swagger stick—an old habit that his critics might have condemned as too British.

SOURCE. *Douglas Botting and the editors of Time-Life Books,* The Second Front (World War II). *Alexandria, VA: Time-Life Books, 1978, p. 80.*

commander. Churchill gave in and issued the necessary orders.

By and large, historians agree that Eisenhower's leadership leading up to the D-Day invasion was masterful and that the decisions he made were the right ones: to select Normandy, rather than Pas de Calais, as the invasion site; to put U.S. Gen. Omar Bradley rather than U.S.

Gen. George Patton in charge of the First Army; to insist on bombing the French railway system in the weeks prior to the landing; to postpone the invasion, scheduled for 5 June, because of bad weather; and to decide the next day, as he told his staff, "Okay, we'll go." Yet, Eisenhower was not absolutely sure that the invasion would succeed. Prior to D-Day he prepared two brief statements for the press. One, announcing that the invasion had succeeded, was later released; the other, which remained in Eisenhower's pocket, announced that the invasion had failed, that the surviving troops were being withdrawn, and that the decision to send them had been his and his alone.

Montgomery: A Dedicated and Egotistical Professional Soldier

One of the greatest challenges to Eisenhower's concept of teamwork was posed by Gen. [Bernard] Montgomery, who was commander of the land forces deployed on D-Day. As head of the British Eighth Army in North Africa, Montgomery had defeated Rommel's Afrika Corps at El Alamein [in northern Egypt] and had driven the Nazis out of the theater of operations. His later campaigns in Sicily and Italy were less successful, but Montgomery's reputation for brilliance remained untarnished. He was a master of the set-piece battle, where he could marshal his forces and plan their disposition with precision. He was less effective in adapting to changing situations and missed more than one opportunity for victory as a result.

Montgomery was a professional soldier who was utterly dedicated to his job and largely indifferent to all other aspects of life. He cultivated a rather folksy image with his berets and baggy sweaters, and this made him popular with the common soldiers. However, Montgomery's peers and immediate subordinates know him to be cold, brusque, and egotistical to the point of insufferability.

Eisenhower both admired Montgomery's tactical acumen and resented his imperious manner. Montgomery found fault with every battle plan but his own. He criticized Eisenhower's suggestions constantly and not always politely. However, Montgomery did make valuable contributions to the planning for Overlord, and his leadership of his troops during the invasion cannot be faulted—even though he did make his share of errors during the subsequent fighting in France and Germany.

The German Command

The Nazi defense of the French coastline against invasion was commanded by Gen. Rommel, with whom both Eisenhower and Montgomery had contended in the past. Rommel had been a highly decorated infantry lieutenant in World War I. Although never a Nazi Party member himself, Rommel was willing to serve the German Nazi leader Adolf Hitler. . . . Before World War II began, Rommel commanded Hitler's personal bodyguard detachment. Later he rode a tank and held a general's rank while the blitzkrieg (lightning war) raged across France. From there he went to command the Afrika Corps, having early successes but eventual defeat. In January 1944 he was given the job of preparing the western coast of France against the inevitable Allied invasion.

Rommel inspected the defenses and found them woefully inadequate. He immediately ordered the installation of a network of land and sea mines, steel obstacles designed to stop landing craft, and concrete pillboxes with overlapping fields of fire. He also had to make decisions concerning the disposition of troops at his command.

Rommel and von Rundstedt: A Difference of Professional Opinion

Rommel believed that the Allies had to be stopped at the water's edge, if they were to be stopped at all. He wanted to have all his reserve troops stationed close to the coast so that they could be deployed to shore up the defense wherever the Allies attacked. However, on this issue he came into conflict with his immediate superior, Field Marshal Gerd von Rundstedt.

Von Rundstedt was a legend in the German army, the Wehrmacht. Almost seventy years old in 1944, he had retired twice but each time had been called back to active service by Hitler himself. As commander-in-chief of the western front, von Rundstedt was ultimately responsible for the defense against the forthcoming Allied invasion. Although von Rundstedt liked and respected Rommel, von Rundstedt believed that any coastal defense, no matter how well prepared, would only slow the Allies, not stop them. He wanted to hold most of the German reserves well back from the coast, out of range of the Allied naval guns that would be sending in devastating fire from the sea in support of the invasion. Then when the Allies headed inland, von Rundstedt planned to launch a massive counterattack that would crush the invaders.

> As Hitler typically did with his military decisions, Hitler tried to have it both ways.

Unlike Rommel, von Rundstedt believed that the invasion force would almost surely land at Pas de Calais, the usable site that was closest to the British coast.

The two men took their professional disagreement to Hitler himself—neither wanted the whole responsibility resting on his shoulders alone. As Hitler typically did with his military decisions, Hitler tried to have it both ways.

Hitler: Critical Indecision

The Fuhrer (leader) had already made Rommel's job more difficult by mixing the lines of command and authority for those units involved in the defense of the French coast. Although Rommel was nominally in charge of the entire defensive apparatus, Hitler denied him command of the German naval and air forces in the area. Nor did Rommel have the authority to direct the SS (Schutzstaffel, elite guard) Panzer divisions in southern France—they remained under control of Hitler himself. So when presented by his commanders with alternate scenarios of invasion, Hitler decided to cover both possibilities. The result satisfied neither of his commanders. Von Rundstedt was given a reserve to keep inland, but it was half the size that he had requested. Rommel was granted additional troops for the coast, but he considered their numbers and equipment inadequate to the task. Hitler further handicapped his generals on the day of the invasion itself. When the Germans saw that the Allies were landing at Normandy, von Rundstedt urgently requested that Hitler deploy the SS Panzer divisions to that area to support the planned counterattack (Rommel, having been informed that the bad weather meant no invasion was possible, had returned to Germany to celebrate his wife's birthday). However, when von Rundstedt radioed Hitler's headquarters, von Rundstedt was informed that Hitler had taken a sleeping pill and gone to bed, with strict orders that he not be disturbed. By the time Hitler finally released the Panzers, it was too late to make a difference.

Many factors contributed to the Allies' victory and the Germans' defeat on D-Day. The difference in leadership was surely one of them.

D-Day Was the Beginning of the End for Nazi Germany

Nation

The following viewpoint, which appeared in the June 17, 1944, edition of the *Nation* magazine, claims that D-Day is only the beginning of the end of the fight against Nazi Germany. It points out that it will be some time before the people know for sure exactly how successful the landings in France were and the effect they may have on the war plan agreed upon at the 1943 Teheran Conference. Meanwhile, the press and the people need to be on guard against German propaganda claiming German successes and Allied failures. The article contends that German leaders know they could not stop an invasion on the beaches and have a strategic force waiting inland to counter the Allies' next line of attack. It warns that even though German leader Adolf Hitler knows he is not strong enough to win on all fronts simultaneously, he is not ready to acknowledge defeat.

SOURCE. "D-Day: The Beginning of the End," *Nation*, June 17, 1944. Copyright © The Nation. All rights reserved. Reproduced by permission.

June 6, 1944: the beginning of the end for Nazi Germany.

D-Day was hailed with a sense of relief all over the world, but people were quick to realize that a new period of tension lay ahead. Now we must wait again, keeping our nerves under control, for indications that the invasion has succeeded. According to Arthur Krock of the *New York Times*, the High Command expects a lapse of four to five weeks before any conclusive verdict on General [Dwight D.] Eisenhower's operations can be given. By that time the whole design of the grand strategy decided on at the Teheran conference [in 1943] may have emerged. For it must not be forgotten that the landings in France are not an isolated event.

> It must not be forgotten that the landings in France are not an isolated event.

They are linked closely to the drive in Italy, which is developing with such success, to the campaign of [Yugoslav president] Marshal Tito, which may be supplemented by Allied operations in the Balkans, and, finally but most important of all, to the new blows which the Red Army has begun to deliver on the eastern front.

Speculation and Assessment

In the immediate future we can expect plenty of colorful details of the fighting but little news of the kind that will enable us to assess its progress. There will be no release from Allied headquarters of any information that could possibly help the enemy. This involves a risk that the public will pay too much attention to the artfully concocted mixture of fact and fancy that [German minister of propaganda Paul Joseph] Goebbels is serving in generous portions. We can only hope that the press will be careful in handling stories from this source. It was unfortunate, to say the least, that the fall of [the French city of] Caen was headlined on a German say-so when

GERMAN DEFENSES ON NORMANDY

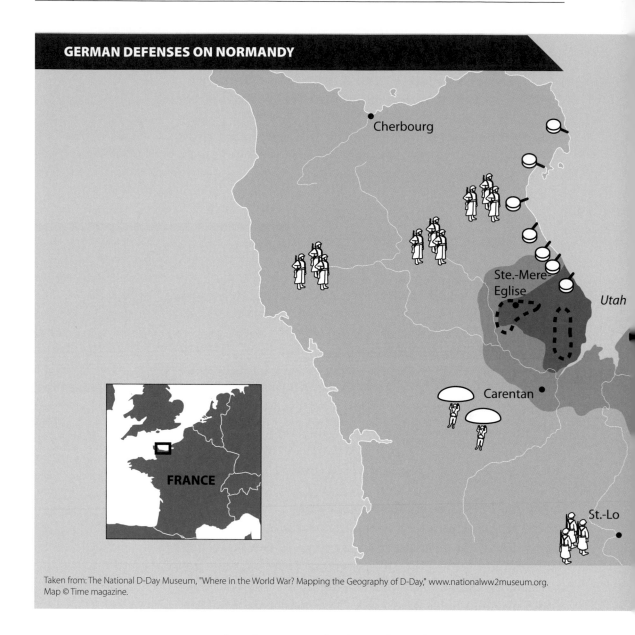

Taken from: The National D-Day Museum, "Where in the World War? Mapping the Geography of D-Day," www.nationalww2museum.org. Map © Time magazine.

next day the papers had to admit that the battle for the town continued.

The broad outline of General Eisenhower's strategy became clear as soon as the location of the first landings were known. It was based upon the geography of the Cotentin Peninsula, which sticks into the English Channel

PERSPECTIVES ON MODERN WORLD HISTORY

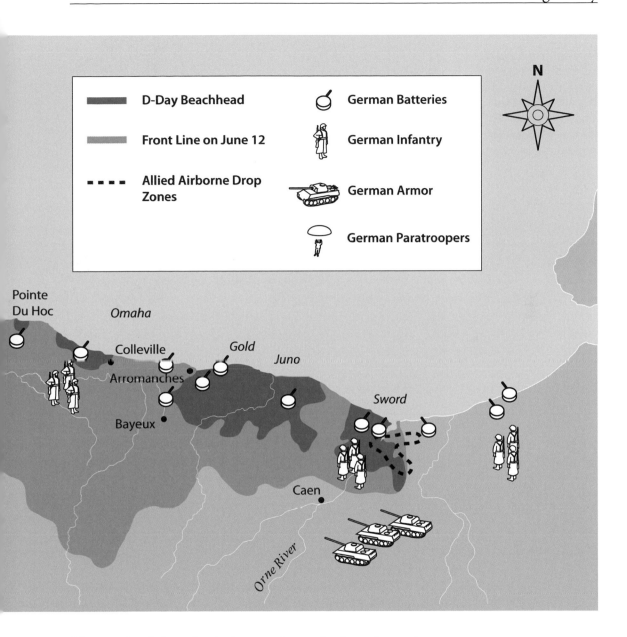

like a raised thumb. At its northern tip, less than ninety miles from the nearest point of the English coast, is the well-equipped deep-water port of Cherbourg. The shores of the peninsula are rocky and unsuitable for landing craft but immediately to the east are the wide sandy beaches of the Bay of the Seine. Here the chief landing—

US soldiers get in position in Cherbourg, an important port for the Allies to conquer in order to establish a base for entry into France. (Fred Ramage/ Keystone/Getty Images.)

to date—was made and a beachhead established cutting the main road and rail communications of Cherbourg. At the same time the peninsula itself was saturated with Allied parachutists whose apparent objective was to isolate Cherbourg and prevent any Nazi reinforcements from reaching it. If this port can be captured the first essential for the deep penetration of France—a good supply base where heavy equipment can be landed—will have been secured.

Rommel's Strategy

Our successes in taking the Normandy beaches proved that a certain amount of bluff had been mixed with the concrete of the Atlantic Wall [a series of German fortifications along the coast of Europe]. In places the first echelons ashore encountered fierce resistance and suffered heavy casualties, but the fixed defenses proved much less formidable than Nazi propaganda had suggested. This does not mean, however, that [German] Marshals [Gerd von] Rundstedt and [Erwin] Rommel have shot their bolt. Whatever Goebbels may have said, they have known all along that they could not stop an invasion on the beaches, and accordingly they have concentrated their best troops well inland as a mobile, strategic reserve to be hurled at the Allies once it is clear where the main line of attack is developing.

The next crisis of the invasion, which may come before these words appear in print, will arise when this élite German force is put in motion. However, Rommel must be sure that Normandy is really the danger point before he can afford to counter-attack there. He knows that only a fraction of General Eisenhower's forces are engaged so far, and the Allied warning to fishermen from Norway to the Pyrenees to stay in port suggests that new landings are contemplated.

But while the Nazi generals wait, the Allied bridgeheads grow stronger. Moreover, the American and British air forces are busy sweeping a wide arc south of the Channel, bombing and shooting up everything German that moves on rail or road, attacking bridges, marshaling yards, stations, barracks, and supply dumps. This war of attrition from the air, together with that carried on by the underground, must be reducing both the mobility and the potential striking power of the Nazi strategic reserve. Yet in the opening stages of the invasion there was little sign of counter-measures by the Luftwaffe [German air force]. In the first two and a half days of the invasion

The Plot to Kill Hitler

The plot to assassinate [German leader] Adolf Hitler on 20 July 1944 was an attempt to overthrow his Nazi regime and end World War II. "Operation Valkyrie" was a plot to take power once the news of Hitler's assassination was confirmed. The bomb meant to kill Hitler was placed in his military headquarters in Rastenberg in East Prussia by a staff officer, Colonel Claus von Stauffenberg. It went off, but its force was muffled by a heavy wooden desk, which saved the Führer's life. Communications from Hitler's headquarters were not severed, and though Stauffenberg made it back to Berlin and tried to rally support, his efforts were doomed from the start. He and the other ringleaders of the plot were quickly caught and shot in the German Ministry of War. Thereafter hundreds of their associates were arrested; most were tortured or executed. For his own enjoyment, Hitler ordered films to be made of their slow deaths by strangulation with piano wire.

This one failed attempt on Hitler's life symbolized the elite character of this part of the German resistance. Most of the plotters were conservative men from prominent families. Many had religious origins and convictions, and they saw it as their mission not only to get rid of Hitler as an abomination but also to save some vestiges of honor for the German people as a whole.

SOURCE. *"July 20th Plot,"* Encyclopedia of Modern Europe: Europe Since 1914: Encyclopedia of the Age of War and Reconstruction, *Vol. 3. New York: Charles Scribner's Sons, 2006, p. 1521. Gale Virtual Reference Library. Copyright © 2006 Gale, Cengage Learning.*

Allied planes flew 27,000 sorties with a loss of little more than 1 per cent. What remains of the Luftwaffe is being hoarded, perhaps for a blow to be synchronized with Rommel's counterattack.

Hitler's Fear and Dilemma

The dilemma of the German western command is but one phase of the total dilemma which total warfare has become for [German leader Adolf] Hitler. Now his old nightmare has become grim reality. Germany is encircled, forced to fight not merely on two but on four fronts. Indeed, we may say on five, for while external foes batter down the walls of Fortress Europe [Nazi-occupied areas of continental Europe], unarmed but increasingly formidable enemies fight within its gates. The strength Hitler commands is still great but not great enough to beat all his challengers at once. Where, then, shall he throw his reserves? Into the western breach and have nothing left to bolster the east when the Red Army strikes? Or must he stem the Russian tide at all costs even though it means opening a path to the Rhine? Again, how far can he strip his home garrisons when Germany harbors ten million foreign slaves waiting a chance to break their bonds?

> Facing defeat, Hitler will fight hard and cunningly. We must be prepared to withstand hard knocks.

Facing defeat, Hitler will fight hard and cunningly. We must be prepared to withstand hard knocks, to suffer setbacks, to avoid diplomatic booby traps. But we have arrived at the beginning of the end, and only a suicidal disruption of the United Nations can rob us of victory.

CHAPTER 3

Personal Narratives

An Infantry Soldier Reflects on D-Day

Robert Rogge

In the following viewpoint, an American veteran explains why in 1941 he, at twenty years of age, joined the Canadian army. He tells how much he wanted to go to England and about the training he and the others in his regiment underwent after arriving there. He goes on to depict the movement of troops, supplies, and vehicles to the assembly areas for embarkation, detailing the soldiers' daily routine, their equipment, and their feelings. He tells what it was like onboard the large infantry landing crafts and how he and his fellow soldiers felt during the landings and afterwards. He shares his feelings about German soldiers in general and the SS Panzer division of Hitler Youth that attacked his group. Robert Rogge served with both the Canadian army and the US Air Force and is the author of *Fearsome Battle: With the Canadian Army in World War II Europe.*

Photo on previous page: The World War II Normandy American Cemetery and Memorial contains the graves of 9,386 troops on a cliff overlooking Omaha Beach and the English Channel in Colleville-sur-Mer, France. **(Mychele Daniau/AFP/Getty Images.)**

Many Americans went to Canada before Pearl Harbor. We did not go there to avoid military service, but to enlist and take an active part in the war against fascism. We had a deep personal desire to fight Adolf Hitler, help save the civilized world and perhaps experience a little bit of adventure. . . . I quit my job in August 1941, went to Montreal and enlisted in the Black Watch of Canada.

On Sunday, December 7, 1941, I was in advanced infantry training at Farnham, Quebec. . . .

From Training in England to Wire-Encircled Camps

When we arrived in England to prepare for the eventual return to Western Europe, our training included schemes to test our skills at exiting landing craft in the proper order, generating artillery cover fire and enduring long-distance marches. . . .

> Along with tens of thousands of other Allied troops, I was prepared as well as possible for the invasion.

Throughout 1942–43, the training intensified in preparation for the coming invasion. Along with tens of thousands of other Allied troops, I was prepared as well as possible for the invasion. After many months with the Black Watch, in December 1943 I transferred to the Stormont, Dundass & Glengarry Highlanders—"the Glens"—a Canadian Scottish unit that had been recruited from around Ontario. . . . Training with my new regiment included exercises with bicycles. . . . We trained for many months on lightweight Raleighs and nearly drove our quartermaster mad with endless requisitions for tires, tubes, patching kits, handlebars, wheels, pedals, chains and sometimes whole bikes. The exercises continued apace throughout the first months of 1944 until May, when we began to make final preparations for the movement to our embarkation areas.

The movement of troops, supplies and vehicles to the assembly areas began in mid-May, and we called it "the sausage machine." It removed us from scattered billets that we had long occupied and stuffed us into relatively crowded wire-encircled camps. Our mail was censored, and armed military policemen patrolled the wire perimeters. Nobody was allowed out of the camps.

A Heavy Weight: Invasion Equipment

All the stuff that men had accumulated during their time in England was left behind when we went into the pre-invasion camps. We stripped down to combat gear and lived out of our small packs. Even so, each man went into the invasion heavily weighted down. He had his Enfield rifle, two Bren machine-gun magazines, five grenades, three bandoliers of ammunition, spare socks and shirt, extra underwear, towel, gas cape, gas mask, ground sheet, two 24-hour ration packs, a fighting knife and a large pocket knife.

Our web equipment included two large pouches in front to hold the Bren magazines, a small pack on our back, canteen on the right hip and bayonet on the left. The small pack held our mess gear, spare clothing, soap, ration packs, cigarettes, writing pad, sewing kit, a canvas roll holding shaving gear, toothbrush and paste, a metal mirror and boot brushes. A small, squarish container held the gas mask and was slung over whatever shoulder was available. A rubberized ground sheet was rolled up under the flap of the small pack, and on top of it was a chemically treated, camouflaged cloth anti-gas cape that could be unrolled by pulling a slip-knotted string. . . .

Although intended to carry ammunition, the front pouches instead held such vital things as cigarettes, socks, matches and toilet paper. Each Bren gunner had an assistant who, in addition to his own rifle, carried a spare barrel, tool kit and two metal boxes, each holding 10 30-round magazines. Thus equipped, the Canadian soldier went ashore on D-Day, and if he was in the 9th Brigade, he toted a bike as well. When one enterprising private weighed all his gear, it tipped the scales at 78 pounds, excluding his helmet, bike and rations.

Life in the Assembly Areas

In the assembly areas our days were spent cleaning our weapons and listening to lectures on what we would face when we confronted the Germans. We were issued two one-day ration packs containing blocks of compressed tea, sugar and dried milk, meat and vegetable stew, bouil-lon cubes, a few sheets of coarse gray toilet paper, hardtack, hard candies wrapped in cellophane and chocolate bars with raisins. . . .

> Next we were briefed on the landing areas, and we were scared witless.

Next we were briefed on the landing areas, and we were scared witless. . . . Plans called for us to land on Juno Beach immediately behind the 7th and 8th brigades, our sister brigades in the 3rd Canadian Division. We were to land at the village of Bernires-sur-Mer and assist the other brigades of the division as we pushed on toward [the French city of] Caen's Carpiquet airfield, our D-Day objective.

After showing us the relief map of the beach, they briefed us on the air and sea strikes that would precede our landings. There would be tons of bombs and naval gunfire from 6-inch to 15-inch guns that, they assured us, would flatten the German defenses. There would be airstrikes and rocket-firing assault ships to drench the beaches with fire just before we touched down. We would have naval officers with us to coordinate the gun-fire from the ships. Our fears began to fade away, but the men who had been sent to us from the 1st Canadian Division—men who had made the landings in Sicily and Italy—knew better: They called the beaches "the bitches."

At the "hards," specially strengthened areas of the ports where the landing craft nosed ashore, we were once again embroiled in that old army game—hurry up and wait. . . .

Almost Embarkation

The day before we embarked we were paid in French occupation francs and given French phrase books. After an early breakfast the next morning, we put on our web gear, clapped on our helmets, slung our rifles and climbed into the trucks that would take us to the ships. . . .

Miles of reinforced roads led to the ports, and lining these roads were yard after yard of wheeled and tracked vehicles. Fields were jammed with tanks, bulldozers, trucks, guns, jeeps, trailers—and ambulances. Artillery shells were also stacked under sheets of corrugated iron alongside the roads, and there were hundreds of acres of other supplies covered with tarpaulins. If we could not break into Europe with all that backing us, we thought, then nobody could. Southern England was so choked with armies and all their gear and supplies that we used to claim that the barrage balloons were the only things that kept it from sinking into the sea.

Seven infantry and three airborne divisions would launch the invasion between the Orne River to the east and the town of Valognes to the west, a front of some 45 miles. The airborne divisions, two American and one British, would secure the flanks. We had been told that there would be more than 4,000 assault ships. The enormity of the whole operation was beyond our comprehension, but we now believed that we would succeed. . . .

Now we were ordered to board the ships. Military policemen patrolled the area and movement control officers, wearing red staff collar badges and armed with megaphones, chased us aboard the landing craft. . . .

The 9th Brigade was onboard LCI(L)s (landing crafts, infantry, large). They had a cleated ramp down each side of the bow on which we would climb down into the water when the time came. The captain of our ship, however, promised us a dry landing.

On Board the LCI

The LCIs had tiered bunks, a novelty to men used to the slung hammocks found on British transports during training. Once on board, we were issued inflatable life jackets that made nice pillows, but we doubted they would hold us up in the water because we had so much gear on us. . . .

Once we had boarded the LCI(L), we were more isolated than we had been in the wired camp. Each ship was a little world of its own. . . . We had been issued "bags, paper, greased, vomit" and some men were already filling theirs but it was not the sea that made their stomachs roil. Each of us was beset by the same thoughts every untried infantryman has had: Will I stand it? Will I cut and run? . . .

> There was no turning back now; the only way off that ship was down the ramps and into the surf.

There was no turning back now; the only way off that ship was down the ramps and into the surf. And yet we were proud to be there. We sang our marching songs, shouted epithets at everything German. We were boosting our morale to face the unknown. . . .

When dawn came, gray and cold, the broadsides delivered by the Allied fleet were stunning. Great clouds of reddish brown smoke rolled downwind, and we could hear the shells howling off into the distance as they sought targets farther inland. Cruisers and destroyers lashed at the coastal defenses, and field artillery batteries onboard ships added to the racket. In the bow of our ship, sailors clamped an ammunition drum onto the 20mm cannon, and pointed its barrel at France.

The Landing

We checked our rifles for the thousandth time and sweated in the cold air. For each of us, our entire being was focused on the landing, for we could clearly see the turmoil on the beaches as the first two brigades of the division landed near Bernieres-sur-Mer, the town where we too would land. . . .

The first men of our division to go ashore found that the preliminary bombardments and shelling had not flattened the defenses as promised, and they were fighting hard to clear the town so that we could land. When the men of the Queen's Own Rifles and the North Shore Regiment landed in front of Bernieres-sur-Mer, a withering German fire met them. Members of the initial assault platoons suffered heavy casualties, but by 9:30 A.M. they had secured the town. . . .

When our brigade landed, we half walked, half-slid down the ramps and into the water. As we hit the water we were star-tied to hear the sound that inspires every Scotsman. Our pipers were playing us ashore to "Bonnie Dundee," our regimental song, as we waded through chest-deep water toward dry land.

> Following orders, we dumped our bikes in designated piles in the streets, hunched our rifle slings higher on our shoulders and followed our officers into France.

On Dry Land

The town was like a lot of seaside towns we had come to know in Britain—some half-timbered houses among others of brick and stone. Narrow, crowded streets were filled with troops and equipment. A Norman church steeple rose up over it all. Meanwhile, the air vibrated with naval gunfire, shore batteries exploding like the slamming of steel doors, machine-gun fire rippling through it all. The intermittent crackle of rifle fire and the dull whump of grenades came to us as we straggled up the stony beach and through the gap in the sea wall and into the town. Dead Germans and Canadians lay there, waxen-faced. We cursed our ship's captain. Dry-shod! We were lucky to have gotten ashore dry-headed. Water squished out of our boots and ran out of our soaked uniforms. . . .

Following orders, we dumped our bikes in designated piles in the streets, hunched our rifle slings higher on our shoulders and followed our officers into France. German signs bearing the warning Achtung Minen [Attention—Mines] hung on barbed wire fences around fields, and we found a couple of smoking Sherman tanks, with the stench of cooked meat still heavy in the air.

We finally arrived at Beny-sur-Mer, a little village a mile or so inland, and were told to stop. That was as far as we were going that day. . . . We moved into an orchard, spread out, sat down and took off our boots and socks. The damned war would just have to wait a minute while we changed into dry socks. Then we brewed up tea. . . . We were ordered to dig in and we got at it. . . . A mortar bomb whispered down and exploded, killing our first man. . . . Others were wounded, and the bandsmen, now acting as stretcher-bearers, quickly got the wounded back to the regimental aid post and on their way to England. . . .

Formidable Enemies: The Hitler Youth

After a brief rest at Beny-sur-Mer, we were ordered to advance on Villon les Buissons, three miles from Caen. . . . It was at Villon les Buissons that we were first attacked by the murderous young psychopaths of the 12th SS Panzer Division Hitlerjugend (Hitler Youth). . . . The Hitler Youth were brutal soldiers who routinely shot unarmed POWs [prisoners of war], the wounded on the battlefield, even German troops who showed signs of quitting. The typical German soldier was a tough customer in his own right, but for me the SS were beyond the reach of human understanding. Over the course of the next several days [the] young soldiers battered themselves against our lines, and although we had suffered only one casualty on D-Day itself, by the morning of the 9th our battalion had been reduced to 200 men.

We would continue to struggle against these youngsters for another month before finally reaching our D-Day objective and capturing Caen.

A German Officer Serves in Normandy

Hans von Luck

In the following viewpoint, a German veteran relates what happened as he and his adjutant kept vigil the night before D-Day not far from the Normandy port city of Caen. He explains the effect the sitting, watching, and waiting for a night exercise to end and an Allied invasion to begin had on him and on his troops. He tells what orders he gave and describes the actions he took upon learning that Allied paratroopers were dropping and gliders were landing nearby. He goes on to describe his frustration, mounting anger, and despair when in spite of all his efforts he could not get clearance from the German High Command for his troops to counterattack. Hans von Luck served in the German armored forces during World War II. He became one of the youngest colonels in the German army and was awarded two of Germany's highest awards for gallantry.

SOURCE. Hans von Luck, "15: The Start of the Invasion, 6 June 1944," *Panzer Commander: The Memoirs of Colonel Hans von Luck*, Praeger Publishers/Random House, 1991, pp. 171–174. Copyright © Estate of Hans von Luck. All rights reserved. Reproduced by permission.

The evening of 5 June 1944 was unpleasant. Normandy was showing its bad side; during the day there had been rain and high winds.

I was sitting in a sparsely furnished house on the edge of the village of Bellengreville, a few kilometers west of Vimont, a small town east of Caen, the industrial center and port of the Normandy coast; before me were papers and maps to do with exercises I was preparing for my regiment. My adjutant, Lieutenant Helmut Liebeskind, was at the command post in the village. I was a major, thirty-two years old. I was to be promoted to lieutenant-colonel at the end of July, and after a further two months to colonel—rapid progress, it seemed to me.

Watching and Waiting

The general weather conditions, worked out every day by naval meteorologists and passed on to us by division, gave the "all clear" for 5 and 6 June. So we did not anticipate any landings, for heavy seas, storms, and low lying clouds would make large-scale operations at sea and in the air impossible for our opponents.

That evening, I felt our lot was highly unsatisfactory: like most of my men, I was used to mobile actions, such as we had fought in the other theaters of war; this waiting for an invasion that was undoubtedly coming was enervating.

But, in spite of the inactivity, morale among the troops remained high, the more so since Normandy spoiled us with butter, cheese, "*crème fraîche*," and meat, as well as cider.

Battalion Activities and Orders

On that rainy evening, my adjutant and I were waiting for a report from No. II Battalion that the night exercise had ended. This battalion was in the area Troarn-Escoville, hence fairly near the coast, while No. I Battalion, equipped with armored personnel carriers

> About midnight, I heard the growing roar of aircraft, which passed over us.

and armored half-track vehicles, had taken up waiting positions further to the rear. I had given the more basic order that in the event of possible landings by Allied commando troops, the battalions and companies concerned were to attack immediately and independently; and to do so, moreover, without regard to the prohibition from the highest authority on engaging action except after clearance by High Command West. But in view of the weather report that we had been given, I had no thought of such an engagement that night.

About midnight, I heard the growing roar of aircraft, which passed over us. I wondered whether the attack was destined once again for traffic routes inland or for Germany herself. The machines appeared to be flying very low—because of the weather? I looked out the window and was wide awake; flares were hanging in the sky. At the same moment, my adjutant was on the telephone, "Major, paratroops are dropping. Gliders are landing in our section. I'm trying to make contact with No. II Battalion. I'll come along to you at once."

I gave orders without hesitation, "All units are to be put on alert immediately and the division informed. No. II Battalion is to go into action wherever necessary. Prisoners are to be taken if possible and brought to me."

Dealing with a Dangerous Situation

I then went to the command post with my adjutant. The 5 Company of No. II Battalion, which had gone out with blank cartridges, was not back yet from the night exercise—a dangerous situation. First reports indicated that British paratroops had dropped over Troarn. The commander of No. II Battalion had already started a counterattack with uninvolved elements and had succeeded in penetrating as far as Troarn, to which elements of the

5th Company had already withdrawn under their own steam.

We telephoned the company commander, who was in a cellar. "Brandenburg, hold on. The battalion is already attacking and is bound to reach you in a few moments." . . .

In the meantime, my adjutant telephoned the division. General Feuchtinger and his general-staff officer had not come back yet. We gave the orderly officer . . . a brief situation report and asked him to obtain clearance for us for a concentrated night attack the moment the divisional commander returned.

> The clearance for an immediate night attack, so as to take advantage of the initial confusion among our opponents, had still not come.

The Non-Ending Issue of Clearance

Gradually we were becoming filled with anger. The clearance for an immediate night attack, so as to take advantage of the initial confusion among our opponents, had still not come, although our reports via division to the corps and to Army Group B ([Field Marshal Erwin] Rommel) must have long since been on hand. We made a thorough calculation of our chances of successfully pushing through to the coast and preventing the formation of a bridgehead, or at least making it more difficult. . . .

The hours passed. We had set up a defensive front where we had been condemned to inactivity. The rest of the division . . . was equally immobilized, though in the highest state of alert. My adjutant telephoned once more to division. Major Forster, IC [intelligence officer] and responsible for the reception of prisoners, came to the phone. He too was unable to alter the established orders. Army Group B merely informed us that it was a matter of a diversionary maneuver: the British had thrown out straw dummies on parachutes. At daybreak, I sent my adjutant to ask divisional command post to secure us immediate clearance for a counterattack . . . But clearance was strictly denied.

[German leader Adolf] Hitler, who used to work far into the night, was still asleep that early morning.

At the command post, I paced up and down and clenched my fists at the indecision of the Supreme Command in the face of the obvious facts. . . .

The Beginning of the End

So the tragedy took its course. After only a few hours, the brave fighting units in the coastal fortifications could no longer withstand the enemy pressure, or else they were smashed by the Allied naval guns; while a German panzer division, ready to engage, lay motionless behind the front and powerful Allied bomber formations, thanks to complete air superiority, covered the coastal divisions and Caen with concentrated attacks. In the early hours of the morning, from the hills east of Caen, we saw the gigantic Allied armada, the fields littered with transport gliders and the numerous observation ballons over the landing fleet, with the help of which the heavy naval guns subjected us to precision fire.

The situation forced us to regroup. Strong combat units were formed on either side of the Orne [River], east and west. We continued to wait for clearance for a counterattack. In view of this superiority, I thought, on seeing the landing fleet, there was no longer much chance of throwing the Allies back into the sea. Bringing up reserves was even now extremely difficult for us. The "second front" had been established. The enemy in the east pressing with superior strength, the ceaseless bombing of our most important industrial centers and railway communications—even the bravest and most experienced troops could no longer win this war. A successful invasion, I thought, was the beginning of the end.

A Journalist Goes Airborne with the Allied Forces

David Woodward

In the following viewpoint, a British journalist describes the scene the day before D-Day as the blackened-faced men of a British parachute unit paraded off to war dressed in camouflage. He tells how parachutists and gliders carrying Allied troops, equipment, and weapons took off from airfields all over the United Kingdom, all part of the same mission. He goes on to describe the reactions of the people in the French villages where the Allies landed on D-Day; the German prisoners, soldiers, and attacks; and the unremitting activity of the invasion itself. David Woodward was the main war correspondent for the *Times* (London) and *Manchester Guardian* from 1944 to the end of World War II. He went on to serve as first secretary in the British legation of the public information department of UNESCO and later as a producer for BBC Radio.

SOURCE. David Woodward, "Airborne Troops Landed Behind Enemy Lines: Attack Began on D-Day Minus One," *Manchester Guardian*, June 9, 1944. http://guardian.co.uk. Copyright © Guardian News & Media Ltd 1944. All rights reserved. Reproduced by permission.

A British parachute unit formed part of the Allied airborne force which was the spearhead of the Second Front. It was landed behind the German lines, seized vital positions, and then linked up with the Allied forces which had landed on the beaches.

Going to War

British paratroopers with war paint on their faces read slogans chalked on a glider plane in June 1944, after Allied forces stormed the Normandy beaches. **(AFP/Getty Images.)**

I watched the unit go to war at dusk on D-1 (the day before D-Day), parading with everybody, from its brigadier downwards, in blackened faces and wearing the camouflage smocks and rimless steel helmets of the air-borne forces. Each of the black-faced men appeared nearly as broad and as thick as he was tall by reason of the colossal amount of equipment which the parachutist carries with him.

The brigadier and the lieutenant colonel made brief speeches. 'We are history,' said the colonel. There were three cheers, a short prayer, and in the gathering darkness they drove off to the aerodromes with the men in the first lorry [truck] singing, incredible as it seems, the notes of the Horst Wessel song [Nazi Party anthem] at the tops of their voices. The words were not German.

It was nearly dark when they formed up to enter the 'planes, and by torchlight the officers read to their men the messages of good wishes from General [Dwight D.] Eisenhower and General [Bernard] Montgomery.

> The parachutists had been busy, and the inhabitants of the little French villages near where the landings took place awoke to find themselves free again.

Then from this aerodrome and from aerodromes all over the country, an armada of troop-carrying planes protected by fighters and followed by more troops aboard gliders took the air.

An Airborne Operation Underway

The weather was not ideal for an air-borne operation, but it was nevertheless decided to carry it out. The Germans would be less likely to be on their guard on a night when the weather was unfavourable for an attack.

First came parachutists, whose duty it was to destroy as far as possible the enemy's defences against an air landing. Then came the gliders with the troops to seize various points, and finally more gliders carrying equipment and weapons of all kinds. Out of the entire force of 'plane which took the unit into action, only one tug and one glider were shot down.

By the time the glider on board which I was had landed, it was very nearly daylight, and the dawn sky was shot with the brilliant yellows, reds, and greens from the explosions caused by the huge forces of Allied bombers covering the sea-borne attack, which was about to begin.

A force of Lancasters [British bombers] . . . put out of action a German battery which otherwise would have made the landing of troops on that beach impossible.

French Reactions

Meanwhile the parachutists had been busy, and the inhabitants of the little French villages near where the landings took place awoke to find themselves free again. In little knots they gathered at windows and at street corners and watched us. They were a little shy and a little reserved for the most part, probably because they remembered Mr. [Winston] Churchill's statement that feint landings would take place, and they reflected that if what they were watching was a feint then the withdrawal of the British troops would mean that they would be responsible once again for their actions to [German SS commander Heinrich] Himmler and [French politician and German collaborator Pierre] Laval.

These considerations did not affect some of them, however. One elderly Frenchman walked into a cemetery where British wounded were being collected amongst grotesque examples of French funerary art and laid upon the stretcher of one of the most seriously wounded men a huge bunch of red roses—an unwittingly appropriate tribute to the wounded men.

The German Troops

Other paratroops told me that as they marched through a small village which had just been devastated by Allied air bombardment they were cheered by French men and women standing among the still smoking ruins of their homes. As D-Day went on it was possible for us, studying the maps at the headquarters of the air-borne division, to see the very high degree of successful surprise which the unit had achieved. German officers were captured in their beds in several places, and it became clear that the anti-air-landing precautions were not nearly as thorough as the Germans had been trying to make out for the past two years.

German prisoners proved a very mixed bag. The Reichsdeutsche [German citizen] was usually either a boy in his teens or an elderly veteran of the last war. There were some units of Volksdeutsche [Germans] who had had German nationality forced upon them after the Hitlerian [Nazi] conquests of Poland and Czechoslovakia, as well as a number of Italians. The generally poor quality of these troops was not unexpected, and it was realised that behind them lay some of the best units of the German Army ready to counter-attack.

The Allies: Fighting Back

As our men prepared to meet these counter-attacks they were continually harried by snipers, who fought with great resolution until they were killed or until their ammunition was exhausted.

Later German tanks and Panzer Grenadiers in armoured lorries began their attack. In theory paratroops, because of their lack of heavy equipment, are considered light-weights for this kind of work, but these men stood up to the Germans just the same. When the fighting was at its most critical a large force of gliders carrying reinforcements flew right into the battle zone and, circling round, landed their cargoes in spite of continued German shelling of the landing zone.

> We could see where the beachhead was long before we got there by the clumps of barrage balloons flying over the ships which lay off the shore.

These gliders turned the tide, and next morning it was an easy matter for us to drive in a captured car from the positions held by the air-borne forces to the beachhead formed by the troops from the sea. The countryside looked empty, but it still looked like posters advertising summer holidays in Normandy.

Small bodies of British troops moved along under cover of woods and hedges. Here and there were the discarded parachutes of our troops. Scattered over the ground were the black shapes of our gliders, most of which had been damaged in one way or another in their landings, with wings or tails sticking up at odd angles.

The Scene at the Beachhead

We could see where the beachhead was long before we got there by the clumps of barrage balloons flying over the ships which lay off the shore. Material already landed was being moved forward in ducks [six-wheel amphibious vehicles] or lorries, or concentrated where it would be best hidden from the air. Mine-clearing operations were going on through the streets of a typical small French seaside resort, with occasional actions between our patrols and German snipers. In one corner of the village lay several German miniature tanks, all put out of action.

Down on the narrow beach, transport moved over wire netting, shifting the stores, and on huts and tents the usual rash of British military initials had already broken out. Up to their chests in the surf, troops were wading ashore from the landing craft. Out in the middle distance were supply ships and destroyers, while the background of the picture was provided by two big battleships slowly, purposefully shelling German positions with their heavy guns.

These guns had already supported the air-borne landings far inland and had badly damaged the local section of the 'Atlantic Wall,' which consisted at this place of medium-sized concrete block-houses and minefields. The Germans had left in such a hurry that they had not removed the mine warnings which they had put up for their own troops so that our work was made simpler by our having the minefields clearly labelled.

A beach dressing station was full of men, British and Germans, mostly lightly wounded. In one corner there I

saw a German N.C.O. [noncommissioned officer] showing to three British soldiers a set of picture postcards he
had bought in Paris representing the principal buildings
of the town.

Back to England

The pilots of the gliders which had done so well the
day before were embarking in an infantry landing-craft
for England to get more gliders to bring over. Having
become a casualty, I travelled with them across the [En-
glish] Channel, which in places seemed literally crowded
with ships making their way along the swept channels
through the German minefields.

The glider pilots landed this morning at one of the
ports used to receive men during the [1940] evacuation
[of Allied soldiers] from Dunkirk [France]. One of the
glider lieutenants told me he had been brought there at
that time. 'The people cheered us then,' he said, 'and now
they just watch us go by. Do you suppose the English ever
cheer their victories?'

A Normandy Teen Experiences the Invasion Firsthand

Louis de Vallevielle

In the following viewpoint, Louis de Vallevielle describes what he heard and saw during the night the Allies landed and how the Germans on his family's property and in his neighborhood reacted. He explains that because the Germans had forbidden his family to walk through the fields of their farm, they did not know the position of the German battery of guns targeted by the Allies. He talks about the fear they felt the first time his family was shelled and about what prompted his brother to leave the safety of their house. He goes on to describe what happened to his brother, why it happened, and how his brother escaped death. At the time of the Allied D-Day invasion, Louis de Vallevielle was a teenager who lived at Brecourt Manor, his family's small farm located several miles from Utah Beach, one of the invasion sites.

SOURCE. Louis de Vallevielle, "The Guns of Brecourt," *Voices of D-Day: The Story of the Allied Invasion Told by Those Who Were There*, Louisiana State University Press, 1994, pp. 194–197. Copyright © Louisiana State University Press. All rights reserved. Reproduced by permission.

Some person came through the flooded area out at about six in the morning, coming through this swamp, and said all of the sea is covered by boats. And we believed it was a joke. So, we had the German guns in the vicinity, but we don't see them, because of the hedgerow, and because it was about three hundred yards away, and the Germans in [our] house threw down their guns, and we did not see them again. And we believed there were no more Germans in the neighborhood. We heard fighting by rifle, by machine gun, but in some different direction, not always in the same direction.

In the early morning, my father wanted to know what had happened. So he asked people, "What is happening?" and was told, "There is parachutists, monsieur." My father said, "Oh, that's nothing," but was told, "Oh, they are very many. Very many."

Sounds and Sights in the Dark

During the night I'd seen a parachute with a light like the middle of the day. Maybe it was one or two hours in the morning. I don't know. I don't know. But very beautiful.

I was asleep. I slept through the night. We had heard the aerial bombing on the coast, but after the bombing, we went to bed. And then we came out of bed when we heard fighting by rifle in the dark, and it was the dropping of parachutists, but we did not know. We hear about that because one German soldier said, "Don't go out of your house. There are many parachutes." And they put their horses and the wagon, because they were yet horse drawn, in the little road, under the trees, not very far from the guns, and they passed all the night like that. And we were in the house—without moving. And in the morning when I woke up, my father said, "Don't go near the window. Things are

> 'It is a machine gun in front of the house in the field.'

happening, because I heard some shots." And he pulled me from the window like that. "It is a machine gun in front of the house in the field. Don't look by the window."

A German then asked my father, did we have a window for directing the gun? And my father said, "No, there are no windows," and he did not insist, and he left.

Trying to Stay Safe

There were other civilians who were refugees here from [the hamlet of] Le Grand-Chemin, and they came with us into the house and we passed all the morning in the corner of the house at the opposite corner, where the German had their office, but now in the office there were two German wounded, and my mother gave them some coffee, and we then saw six Germans come in the courtyard, drinking some water, to the pump, and then went away to the rear. So we believed there were no more Germans.

It was seven or maybe eight o'clock, and again more fighting. Noise, with machine guns, with grenades, from different directions. And we believed it was an attack, and we believed it was approaching, and we did not understand, because our opinion was that the Germans were gone. At the time, we received shelling for the first time, and I believed it was a gun of the battery, or something like that, and we were very afraid. And my father put us back in the corner of the cellar, because the walls were very thick, and no window.

After the mortar shelling, troopers knocked at the door, and it was a very large door for the entry in the courtyard, and the two wounded Germans were standing in the road. We don't know if the soldiers were American or British, but we know they cannot be Germans. So we said to each other, "It is necessary to go out, and explain we are French, and we are civilians," and during the time, we grouped together—two or three with wives, one baby, and my brother Michel went out and passed in the neighborhood of the two Germans who were surrounded, and my brother Michel was waving his shirt and he spoke French.

Tragedy Strikes

Just in front of the Germans there were ten parachutists, and behind was the gate of the fields, and farther up the side of the field, there was again another ten parachutists. So Michel came through, and they indicated for him to pass through the gate, and after they closed the gate, they shot him in the back.

> After they closed the gate, they shot him in the back.

He fell down in the field, and he was not visible to us. We did not understand. We cannot explain in American, they cannot explain in French. The trooper was a very big one, and he was very excited. I saw a Tommy gun and bayonet, and they encircled us, and they would not look for identification cards. We offer to show the identification cards, and they say "No, no, no, no, no," and they came to me and they said, "Go this way." And my father stopped and said, "No, don't. Stay with us. If we all stay together, they will do nothing."

One of the women who was a servant was crying, and they believed all were to be killed. Then two of the parachutists came by the gate, close to the courtyard, and came at that side where there were two old people, an old man and his wife, and they brought them out with us. We were held there maybe five minutes, when my father asked for mercy. And then he took his identification card, and most of them did not want to look at cards, but someone came and took the paper, looked at him, and said, "Colored." Was a French colored?

A State of Confusion

And my father told the two troopers who were the most excited to come away. At that time, we found my brother on the other side of the gate, because my mother asked, "Where is Michel?"

He was on the ground, in the grass, and I saw him first, and I asked Michel, "Are you dead?" It was stupid, but like that, I asked, "Are you dead?"

And he answered, "No, but I'm wounded through the chest." And the two parachutists told me, "He is a German. You want we kill him?" And I said, "This man is my brother," and they asked, "Then are you a German?" I said, "No, I'm French," but it was all a state of confusion.

So, they all went away, and did not come back again, but they brought me to my father, and we stayed with him, alone, and lay down with the other civilians, and we did not dare to move, because we knew if some Germans came or some other Americans. . . .

> The tanks moved in and raked the hedgerows surrounding the field to make sure there were no surviving riflemen or machine gunners left.

At this time, the infantry was coming through the road, and it was difficult for the infantrymen because there were a lot of German carriages, wagons, and the dead horses of German carriage. There were thirty dead horses. But in the field where the guns were, I did not see. We could not walk through the fields of the farm, and so therefore, the position of this battery in the field adjacent to our manor, we had never been allowed to go out there. We had no idea exactly where those positions were until after D-Day.

Then other American came, and it was infantry, because their clothes were different. And they were coming by the small road, and they asked us if we were civilians; where were the Germans?

One man spoke French, and he said to me, "Your brother is wounded." They told us there were three thousand boats on the sea. At this time the tanks moved in and raked the hedgerows surrounding the field to make sure there were no surviving riflemen or machine gunners left, but the Germans had withdrawn at this time.

A Life Saved

The infantry came, and we started walking, and there was a priest with a bike. I was very surprised to see a bike. He said some prayers, and when I saw the DD tanks [amphibious Duplex Drive swimming tanks developed for D-Day], I asked for some medical assistance, and they promised me to call a doctor, and in fact, a doctor came in five minutes. Michel had six bullets. So the doctor said it is necessary to take him and bring him to the hospital or he will die tonight.

As he was speaking, Michel said, "I don't want to go to the hospital. I prefer to die here." And my father made the decision again, and so Michel departed with the two medics on a wagon, and then a German force captured the wagon for a while, but we reached the road of the Le Grand-Chemin. At this place, we got the first jeep we saw, but they said, "You cannot go farther, turn back to your house. You will receive some news."

My father gave them some papers to give our exact name, and Michel was taken to first aid assistance, and he received plasma under an apple tree. He received some plasma transfusion. And then he was brought in the ambulance to the hospital, where he stayed twenty-one days at the hospital. This was all because of a mistake, a slip-up not to ask for papers.

A German Paratrooper Prepares for an Attack

Martin Poppel

In the following viewpoint, a German veteran shares entries from his war diary, commenting on the sounds and sights of battle and detailing the happenings from their perspective for June 7–10, 1944. He describes how the operation is conducted each day and reveals his concerns for his fellow soldiers, for the losses his regiment has suffered, and for the unexpected and unexplained changes in battle plans. He laments the lack of men and the condition of some of their equipment in contrast to the Allies' armory of heavy guns and seemingly endless number of ships and unrelenting air power. He goes on to describe the emotions of the men as the battle grinds on and they alternate between failure and success. Martin Poppel was a German paratrooper during World War II and is the author of *Heaven and Hell: The War Diary of a German Paratrooper*.

SOURCE. Martin Poppel, "Soldiering On," *Heaven and Hell: The War Diary of a German Paratrooper*. Copyright © Martin Poppel. Published by Spellmount Publishers, an imprint of The History Press. All rights reserved. Reproduced by permission.

*D*iary, 7 June [1944]

At first light vast numbers of enemy bombers reappear, bringing death and fire into the French hinterland. Naturally, their targets are the railway junctions, strategic concentration points and channels of communication, as well as our advancing armoured units. They know well enough that if they can eliminate our reinforcements they should be able to achieve their objectives without massive casualties. As for our own pilots—they are nowhere to be seen.

A Cause for Concern: The Fate of I Battalion

> We all reckon that I Battalion has been thrown into battle alone and with no prospects of success.

We all reckon that I Battalion has been thrown into battle alone and with no prospects of success. It must already have suffered considerable casualties if it hasn't been wiped out completely. . . . During the night, the Regimental Commander has ordered II Battalion to relieve I Battalion. The northeast position of the hills of St Come-du-Mont must be held at all costs. . . .

Enormous explosions can be heard in the north and northeast, which must be coming from the enemy's naval heavy artillery. We can also hear the noise of battle from that direction.

13.00 hours. 9 Company has now been moved to St Come-du-Mont to consolidate our positions there.

We have learned that I Battalion has suffered very high casualties after the Americans made further airborne landings by glider to the rear of them in the early hours of the morning. With enemy units ahead of them, with a whole Regiment of elite enemy troops behind them, and with marshland to the south, all that the Battalion could do was to take up a position of all-round defence and defend themselves to the last man. Meanwhile,

II Battalion has gone on the attack in the north, but made only sporadic contact with enemy units and has been forced to withdraw to the hills. . . .

During the morning, 9 Company advances as far as the foothills of the mountains but is then forced to yield to the enemy's superior force. The Company is now sealing off the hills alongside units of II Battalion and the infantry.

The Situation at 1700 Hours

17.00 hours. On the order of the Battalion, second mortar group . . . is despatched to reinforce 9 Company. I go with my captured French car and the lorry [truck] over the 2 kilometres of marshland to St Come-du-Mont so that I can supply the group myself. . . .

At Regimental headquarters the order reaches me to prepare tomorrow's attack with Oberleutnant Wagner. The plan is to drive the enemy back to St Marie-du-Mont. In the opinion of the men involved, this task can't be achieved with the forces we have available. The Americans, supported by their naval artillery, are already advancing inexorably and our advanced units are already engaged in bitter fighting. Although night is slowly closing in, there has been no let-up in the noise of battle. . . .

> What has persuaded the Commander to depart from the basic principles of his map exercise?

Despite everything we learned in our peacetime exercises, the men are lying in large groups right next to each other. They can only be dispersed with great difficulty and much profanity. A few hundred metres further on, and the shells are landing close by. At once I'm transported back into the old-style warfare. I come across Wagner behind a hedge, in discussion with the infantrymen. Today he doesn't seem as calm and level-headed as he usually is. . . .

After a short time the main points of the attack have been discussed over the map, the ground signals and signals agreed. . . . Then a cry from ahead: enemy attacking with tanks!

The men, particularly the infantrymen, are damned jittery. But even Wagner can't seem to make up his mind what to do. Since I can't help here but can only make things worse, I start to make the journey back with my lads. At the junction I meet my mortar group, which has just got here by truck. Quickly, we organize the unloading of the shells. I give my instructions . . . and then travel back in the lorry. The driver races along the narrow dirt road with its high hedgerows like the devil incarnate, and brings us back to Regimental HQ [headquarters].

Preparing for an Attack

A massive operation is under way there. . . . Messengers hurry past and are quickly dispatched on their way. The lamp is burning in the underground bunker—the Commander and the Battalion Commander are at work. Outside, the soldiers' cigarettes are glowing in the darkness. The Old Man gives Oberleutnant Prive the information about tomorrow's attack, so he discusses the last details with us. He too is less than delighted with the strength of the forces available to him. . . .

What has persuaded the Commander to depart from the basic principles of his map exercise? Before this he always preached to us to 'Think big!'—but now he's simply tearing this fighting Regiment apart. It's incomprehensible. But perhaps—and more likely—the whole tragedy lay in the fact that the whole Regiment had only about 70 trucks at its disposal, and these were often so old and useless that we couldn't repair them when they broke down. Replacement parts simply weren't available any more. Consequently, most of our elite Regiments had to go everywhere on foot, like in the Middle Ages, carrying all the heavy guns, anti-tank guns and mortars. The

General Staff seems to have thought that we paratroopers could manage with nothing more than our knives. . . .

Battling the Allies

8 June

Things get under way before dawn. Only one thing is wrong: it's not our attack, but the enemy's, hitting deep into our assembled troops. The attack begins with sustained bombardment from the enemy naval artillery, explosion after explosion landing on our comrades over there. Using our field glasses and the battery commander's telescope, we try to penetrate the thick mist, but without success. We can locate the line only roughly by listening for the exceptionally rapid fire of our MG 42s [machine guns]. Our six-barrelled mortars have begun to fire as well, but there's just no comparison with the enemy's armoury of heavy guns.

As the day grows brighter, we can see our targets. At one point there's a large number of Yankees running about, apparently a supply depot or even a command post. . . . We send the first shells over. After a few shots, we start to make direct hits. Brick dust whirls upwards from the farmhouse, people come running out in an attempt to get away from concentrated mortar fire. Even the cows are jumping around in comical fashion. Don't forget—we can shoot too.

> There's nothing we can do except suffer and wait.

On the mountains, the sound of battle is moving to the west—which means that we are retreating slowly. If we could only get a signal from the infantry, but there's nothing, absolutely nothing. It makes me want to throw up. We're desperate to help those poor fellows, but when we've no idea where the front line is we can't do a thing. Surely it would be so easy for the infantry to show the position of the front line by sending up a light signal?

The Awesome Power of the Allies

It's full daylight now. The enemy's artillery strikes are landing further forward, making thick clouds of smoke drift eastwards over the hedges. More gliders are landing by the church of Ste Mere Eglise. . . .

Through the battery commander's telescope we can see the enemy fleet at the mouth of the Vire [River]. An overwhelming spectacle of the power of the Allies. Ship after ship, funnel after funnel—a sight that absorbs everyone with its sheer military strength. Twenty-seven big freighters each with three or more funnels, ten battleships, twenty or thirty cruisers, hundreds of smaller vessels can be recognized and counted. Really, it looks like a naval review in peacetime. We can clearly see the muzzle flashes from the warships, then the heavy stuff screams overhead and tears deep holes in the marshland. There's nothing we can do except suffer and wait.

Once again, the fighter-bomber formations are approaching the town. They're there, their machines scream into the dive. The dreadful crack of bombs on houses, then dirt and dust are thrown into the air and our tower sways. They turn and come in again. Dammit, get down from this scaffold. My God, that only just missed. But it's no good—we have to climb to the top again as it's the only way we can help our hard-pressed comrades in their battle.

After a long time spent in fruitless observation, during which my howitzer platoon leader asks me three times whether he can open fire, we see some units retreating. At first a few men, individually, then whole groups, platoons coming back at the foot of the mountains. The enemy fire is increasing all the time, but we have no real chance of responding effectively. Then, even more bad luck, a barrel burst. Two men—of course, they're the best gunners—are badly wounded and two others less so. A tragic loss considering how few guns we have for the whole Regiment. . . .

A Return to Competency

Meanwhile it has turned into a beautiful day, blue sky, the sun burning hot in the sky. On both sides though, the soldiers continue to suffer. Raiding parties search the city for French vehicles and fuel, and my organizers prove themselves extremely competent once again. A wonderful pale grey limousine rolls up, followed by a little blue one, and we also get our hands on a motorcycle and repair it. . . .

9 June

Now, halfway up the mountain, we can at last see the American infantry units. Well, you fellows, we've been waiting for you for hours. In no time, the order to open fire is given to the howitzer platoon. Shortly afterwards the shooting begins and, after a few corrections, we begin to score direct hits on the Yankees—exactly where we wanted. . . . Suddenly life on this mountain is fun again as we make the Yankees scatter. How our infantry will celebrate, especially those involved in the rearguard action. It's only a shot in the arm from the rascally artillery, but it brings some relief, especially if we can make every shot count. More groups are working their way to the road. 'Rapid rate of fire.' My poor gunners have had long enough to rest. Their aim is excellent and the range-finder operator is already preparing for new targets.

> Suddenly life on this mountain is fun again as we make the Yankees scatter.

1100 Hours: The Battle Continues

11.00 hours. Whole columns of infantry appear on the railway line, heading towards us. It's to be hoped that the Americans don't get too far forward, or they'll be able to attack the lads on the flank. To the left and right of the tracks there's marshland, so no alternative route is available to the retreating Germans. Apparently the Americans haven't spotted them yet though, since they aren't directing any artillery fire at the tracks.

Meanwhile the Americans have advanced to the road and our own infantry has reached the protecting bridge in numbers. Now to send over our heavy stuff. Those fellows really do offer a tempting target. Our six-barrelled mortars . . . open up. The shells land right in the middle of the Yankees. The whole area, including our old command post, is now coming under fire from the guns. Our infantry exploits the situation at once and works its way forward at great speed. It's a miracle that the Americans didn't direct their artillery fire at the road and the railway.

The entire Battalion staff has now joined us in here. . . .

We continue to organize ourselves and to drag whatever we can from [the town of] Carentan. Butter, cheese, real coffee, wine, champagne, socks and shirts—all coveted and needed. The men continue to strengthen the positions, clean their guns and themselves. Ammunition belts are reloaded, 11.00 hours: about twenty amis [friends] can be seen by the old Vire bridges, helping to build footbridges, and there is also considerable activity by supply trucks. Just what our mortars and machine guns have been waiting for. I gladly give permission to open fire.

An American Soldier Remembers Omaha Beach

Chuck Hurlbut

In the following viewpoint, an American veteran describes the atmosphere, camaraderie, and conditions on the boat and the assault craft that took him and his fellow soldiers to the beaches of Normandy. He shares the sights and sounds that surrounded them as they headed for the beach and describes what happened to them and their raft full of explosives as, ducking bombs and gunfire, they waded through ankle-deep water toward the shore. He relates how he felt and what he did to protect himself after finding himself alone on the beach, separated from all of his comrades. He goes on to describe what he did when he finally spotted a group of men at an aid station and what transpired after he joined them. Chuck Hurlbut served in the 299th Combat Engineer Battalion and is a survivor of the D-Day Battle of Omaha Beach.

SOURCE. Chuck Hurlbut, "Omaha Beach Armageddon," tankbooks .com, 2009. www.tankbooks.com. Copyright © Aaron Elson. All rights reserved. Reproduced by permission.

Wé'd waited so long. Here was the big day, and we were attached to the First Division, which is one of the best divisions in the Army. We thought, "Geez, we must be pretty good for them to pick us to accompany them." There were a lot of mixed feelings.

En Route: On an English Ship

We're in the boat. We rendezvous, and we're set on our route. And it's about a hundred miles; they said it will take a few hours. The officers said, "Try to get some sleep," but you couldn't.

Late that night we had a supper. Pretty good food. It was an English ship. They knocked themselves out. Then a bunch of us, old buddies, were in a little room on the ship, and we were having some coffee . . . and a bunch of officers looked in. They said, "Can we join you?" . . .

> All you knew was that there were thousands of boats all around you.

So they joined us, and you never realized they were officers. We all became American guys. We talked about movies, automobiles and girlfriends. Anything but war. . . .

Then we went up on deck, but it was dark. You couldn't see much. All you knew was that there were thousands of boats all around you. You could hear things. Bullhorns. And someplace you could hear a guitar being played. It carries across the water.

Getting Ready for the Trip

Early in the morning, we were told to get ready. . . .

We'd gotten all new o.d.s [olive drab fatigues] and stuff way back . . . and we'd never taken them off, so we're all dressed. But now we had to put on our field jacket. And then these impregnated coveralls; they would stand by themselves they were so stiff. They were impregnated to resist gas. Then on top of that a bandolier of bullets. Your gas mask. An inflatable life belt. Your backpack with your mess kit and some rations and a shovel. Your steel helmet, you made sure it was fastened. And your rifle; we all put condoms over the end of the rifle to keep the water out.

Everybody had to carry a bag of explosives. I had fuse lighters. . . .

Well, you've got fifty, sixty pounds of equipment, you could hardly move. . . .

Then somebody yelled, "Get up on deck!" . . .

The guys had all gathered along the rail, the different groups, and we just kidded each other, wisecracked, got a lot of addresses. Wished everybody good luck. Then we went down the cargo net. We had practiced that, and no matter how many times you practice it it's always dangerous. The water was so choppy, the assault craft would bang up against the side of the ship and then drift away, and they couldn't keep it there. Sometimes you were laying spreadeagled looking down at the water, then it would let up and you'd straighten up again.

Getting to the Beach

As far as I know, we all made it down into the assault craft, an LCVP [landing craft vehicle personnel], which holds about 30 men. And right in the center is a big rubber raft full of explosives. So we get situated all around the rubber raft. And in the back, the stern, is where the guy steers it, he's a coxswain, and there were two of them. . . . They're gonna steer this thing into the beach. . . .

> And the flash, we lit up like daylight with big orange flashes from the guns, and the noise, my God.

It's about a two-hour run. So it was around 3 o'clock in the morning. We were ten to twelve miles out in the [English] Channel.

Our boat pulled away once it was loaded up and we went to another area and circled, awaiting other craft to line up with us. Then somebody, someplace decided they were lined up and he gave a signal and we took off, heading for the beach.

About this time the big guns open up. The big battleships are behind us. The noise, unbelievable noise. And the flash, we lit up like daylight with big orange flashes from the guns, and the noise, my God. These are big guns. And they're presumably shelling the beach ahead of us. We heard some bombers go over, and presumably they are bombing the beach. And as we proceed, we pass a big flat barge full of rockets, and all of a sudden these rockets, . . . thousands and thousands of rockets head for the beach. And you began to realize, this is gonna be easy. How in the world can anyone survive what they're receiving there? There's going to be nobody alive when we get there. That was the attitude.

The Realities of War

We're still going along, and all of a sudden we pull alongside this LSM [an amphibious warfare ship], the ones that carried the tanks. And we couldn't believe it, because we're still quite a ways out, but all of a sudden they start letting the tanks off. The tanks disappear. You'd think the guy would know something's wrong here. Another one. Straight down. Unbelievable. . . .

But as we passed, the guys started bobbing up to the surface, floating like corks, screaming and yelling. I thought, "Why don't we stop and pull them into our boats?" We just went right by them. Right then I saw that compassion is not part of war. You've got a mission to do, nothing can interrupt it. And as heartbroken as you felt for those guys, you couldn't stop. Other boats were assigned to rescue them. Our mission was to get to the beach and do our job. Nothing could distract us. . . .

The shelling continued, and as we got nearer the beach, a wave of infantry was just ahead of us. . . . They were supposed to keep the snipers down while we do our work. That was the plan.

But in war plans never go right. So when we get in there . . . the water was only about ankle deep where we got off. There are other cases where they let them off way out and they just drowned, with all this equipment. But we got in good, right in the midst of the obstacles.

Just prior to the ramp coming down we could hear the machine guns hitting the ramp, [and] we said, "Hey, something's going on here. We're not supposed to get this."

Loss of a Raft and Explosives

The ramp went down, and we all got off. The raft got off. And the first thing I did—the craziest thing—I took my rifle and I aimed at a pillbox and I fired. . . . Why I did that I don't know, it was an impulse I couldn't control. . . .

The rubber raft was right behind us, so I grabbed a tow rope and started pulling. The raft was full of all our explosives, and I wanted to get it over to where we could use them on the obstacles. And as I pulled it I found it getting heavier. I look around, there's three bodies on it. . . .

So I'm pulling, and all of a sudden a mortar comes over, hits the raft and the whole goddamn thing blows up. I remember seeing thick black smoke and debris flying, and hearing a loud bang, but I guess it blacked me out, and I somersaulted. Next thing I know I'm on my hands and knees, spitting blood, I have the worst headache you can imagine, and my ears are ringing.

Going It Alone

Well, there go all our explosives. I saw a bunch of guys not far away, and I got over to them. An officer was there. He said, "Look, we've lost our explosives. We have nothing to work with. It looks like it's every man for himself. Try to make the beach. We'll have to come back later in the day and do our job." So everybody took off, and we soon became separated. I was soon all by myself.

On the way in, you would go from one obstacle, wait awhile, look around, to another obstacle, all the time getting closer and closer to the dunes. . . .

> "All I could see was chaos, catastrophe."

The sand dune is about three feet high, and I'm sitting against it. It gave you protection from small arms fire, but not from mortars. So I'm crouched up there, shaking, cold, freezing to death, . . . soaking wet, wondering . . . what's going on? What happened to our plan? Trying to make some reason out of this chaos. And all I could see was chaos, catastrophe. Boats burning, smoking, dead men all along the water's edge, floating bodies. Craft getting hit. It was awful, awful, awful. . . .

Moving On

Finally I said, . . . "I've got to try to find some of my guys and try to put some order to something here." Off in the distance, to my right, I could see a congregation of guys and a big Red Cross flag. . . . There's one tank not too far away, burning. I decided I'll make it to the tank. I made it to the tank, sat down behind it. Pretty well protected now. And this gave me another chance, a few minutes, to look out at this confusion all around me. . . . There were some other vehicles between me and this congregation. I'd pick one out, make it to that, sit and rest a while. One was a jeep. The other one was another tank. The tank had smoke pouring out. I didn't want to go up and look to see if there were dead guys. I just hoped they got out. And there's dead bodies all over the place, all along the water, dead. A lot of knocked out vehicles, overturned landing craft. Just chaos.

I made it to this congregation, and there was quite a bunch of guys there. Now the sand dune has petered out to nothing, but some big cliffs have taken over. It's the far western end of the beach. Omaha Beach just sort of abruptly ends, and these cliffs come right down to the water. For that little section there, these cliffs were giving quite a bit of safety. And there were hundreds of guys crowded behind it. Some were bandaged, some were wounded, some with their arm in a sling. But they were all dazed, confused. Some didn't have helmets. Some didn't have rifles. You couldn't imagine, these are American soldiers who a few hours ago were full of spirit and energy and here they are so disarrayed and astonished and stunned they didn't know what the hell they were doing. And in the flat area there were dozens and dozens and dozens of stretchers. It was a pickup aid station. And it seemed like every third guy on a stretcher was one of my buddies. . . . I helped—a lot of us helped—carry them out to the hospital ship which was just offshore. They were carrying them piggyback, in their arms, on stretchers.

> It seemed like every third guy on a stretcher was one of my buddies.

A Brief Interlude of Safety

This is still early in the morning, maybe eight, nine o'clock. But they'd already set up an aid station for the wounded, and they were trying to get them back to the hospital ship which would rush them back to England.

There was a big Red Cross sign, and evidently the Germans recognized the Red Cross. They'd lob one in once in a while, but not a heavy concentration. They acknowledged the Red Cross flag. So it's sort of a semi safe area.

I finally found a rifle. There were hundreds of them to select from, all over, because I'd lost my rifle when the rubber raft exploded. . . . I finally did get one but it was all full of sand so I had to sit down and disassemble it and clean it all up. Then I spotted two or three guys I knew. . . . I went over and joined them. And one of them was a sergeant, so I thought, now at least we've got some leadership. And his advice was, "Stay close, guys, our instructions are not to leave the beach, we're to stay here, and chances are at low tide in the afternoon we're going back out and do the job clearing these obstacles. That's a hell of a thing to look forward to." But he was right, that's what happened.

A Journalist Takes a Walk Along an Invasion Beach

Ernie Pyle

In the following viewpoint, a journalist describes the feelings evoked in him by what he sees as he walks along France's Normandy coast ten days after D-Day. He describes the visible signs of the waste and devastation of war—the boats and other wreckage lying at the bottom of the sea or half-submerged and the debris of all sizes and shapes, from vehicles to rolls of barbed wire, lying high and dry on the beach. He laments their loss and explains why the Allies could afford the loss on D-Day of enough men and machinery for a small war. He goes on to talk about the never-to-be-forgotten expressions he saw on the faces of German prisoners standing on a high bluff contemplating the vast Allied armada below. Ernie Pyle was a widely read war correspondent during World War II who won worldwide recognition for his sympathetic accounts of the average American soldier.

SOURCE. Ernie Pyle, "The Horrible Waste of War," *Ernie's War: The Best of Ernie Pyle's World War II Dispatches*, Random House, 1986, pp. 280–282. Copyright © Ernie Pyle/Random House. Courtesy Scripps Howard Foundation. All rights reserved. Reproduced by permission.

I took a walk along the historic coast of Normandy in the country of France.

It was a lovely day for strolling along the seashore. Men were sleeping on the sand, some of them sleeping forever. Men were floating in the water, but they didn't know they were in the water, for they were dead.

The water was full of squishy little jellyfish about the size of your hand. Millions of them. In the center each of them had a green design exactly like a four-leaf clover. The good-luck emblem. Sure. Hell yes.

> The wreckage was vast and startling.

I walked for a mile and a half along the water's edge of our many-miled invasion beach. You wanted to walk slowly, for the detail on that beach was infinite.

The wreckage was vast and startling. The awful waste and destruction of war, even aside from the loss of human life, has always been one of its outstanding features to those who are in it. Anything and everything is expendable. And we did expend on our beachhead in Normandy during those first few hours.

Along the Water's Edge: A Scene of Carnage

For a mile out from the beach there were scores of tanks and trucks and boats that you could no longer see, for they were at the bottom of the water—swamped by overloading, or hit by shells, or sunk by mines. Most of their crews were lost.

You could see trucks tipped half over and swamped. You could see partly sunken barges, and the angled-up corners of jeeps, and small landing craft half submerged. And at low tide you could still see those vicious six-pronged iron snares that helped snag and wreck them.

On the beach itself, high and dry, were all kinds of wrecked vehicles. There were tanks that had only just

Soldiers survey the wreckage on a beach in Normandy following the D-Day invasion. (Frank Scherschel/Time & Life Pictures/Getty Images.)

made the beach before being knocked out. There were jeeps that had burned to a dull gray. There were big derricks on caterpillar treads that didn't quite make it. There were half-tracks [military vehicles] carrying office equipment that had been made into a shambles by a single shell hit, their interiors still holding their useless equipage of smashed typewriters, telephones, office files.

There were LCT's [landing craft tanks] turned completely upside down, and lying on their backs, and how they got that way I don't know. There were boats stacked on top of each other, their sides caved in, their suspension doors knocked off.

In this shoreline museum of carnage there were abandoned rolls of barbed wire and smashed bulldozers and big stacks of thrown-away lifebelts and piles of shells still waiting to be moved.

In the water floated empty life rafts and soldiers' packs and ration boxes, and mysterious oranges.

On the beach lay snarled rolls of telephone wire and big rolls of steel matting and stacks of broken, rusting rifles.

On the beach lay, expended, sufficient men and mechanism for a small war. They were gone forever now. And yet we could afford it.

We could afford it because we were on, we had our toehold, and behind us there were such enormous replacements for this wreckage on the beach that you could hardly conceive of their sum total. Men and equipment were flowing from England in such a gigantic stream that it made the waste on the beachhead seem like nothing at all, really nothing at all.

The Enormity of It All

A few hundred yards back on the beach is a high bluff. Up there we had a tent hospital, and a barbed-wire enclosure for prisoners of war. From up there you could see far up and down the beach, in a spectacular crow's-nest view, and far out to sea.

And standing out there on the water beyond all this wreckage was the greatest armada man has ever seen. You simply could not believe the gigantic collection of ships that lay out there waiting to unload.

Looking from the bluff, it lay thick and clear to the far horizon of the sea and on beyond, and it spread out to the sides and was miles wide. Its utter enormity would move the hardest man.

As I stood up there I noticed a group of freshly taken German prisoners standing nearby. They had not yet been put in the prison cage. They were just standing there, a couple of doughboys [infantrymen] leisurely guarding them with tommy guns.

The prisoners too were looking out to sea—the same bit of sea that for months and years had been so safely empty before their gaze. Now they stood staring almost as if in a trance.

They didn't say a word to each other. They didn't need to. The expression on their faces was something forever unforgettable. In it was the final horrified acceptance of their doom.

If only all Germans could have had the rich experience of standing on the bluff and looking out across the water and seeing what their compatriots saw.

GLOSSARY

Allies World War II alliance of the United States, Great Britain, Canada, and the Soviet Union.

Atlantic Wall A series of fortifications—including walls, bunkers, minefields, barbed wire fences, trenches, observation posts, artillery positions, beach obstacles, and other defensive constructions—built by the Germans to defend against an Allied invasion and extending more than 3,200 miles along Europe's Atlantic coast.

Axis World War II alliance of Germany, Italy, and Japan.

Battle of Normandy Fighting that took place in Normandy, France, between occupying German forces and invading Allied forces between June 6, 1944 (D-Day) and the end of August 1944.

Cotentin Peninsula Piece of land that juts out into the English Channel from Normandy towards England, forming part of the northwest coast of France; also known as the Cherbourg peninsula.

D-Day Day on which a certain military operation begins or is set to begin; June 6, 1944, the day on which the Allies of World War II invaded Normandy, France.

East Anglia A region of eastern England; the site of many airfields for the Royal Air Force.

Falaise pocket Area between four cities near Falaise, France, that was the scene of a bloody battle between Allied and German forces in August 1944.

Fortress Europe Areas of Continental Europe occupied by the Nazis during World War II.

Gold Beach Code name for one of five designated beaches used during the

D-Day landings; beach assigned to the British for the D-Day invasion.

Junkers 88   German aircraft.

Juno Beach   Code name for one of five designated beaches used during the D-Day landings; beach assigned to the Canadians for the D-Day invasion.

Luftwaffe   German air force.

Omaha Beach   Code name for the largest and most intensely fought-over beach of the five designated beaches used during the D-Day landings; a beach assigned to US forces for the D-Day invasion.

Operation Cobra   Code name for the July 24–25, 1944, breakout attack launched by the United States to overtake German troops in France.

Operation Goodwood   Code name for British general Bernard Montgomery's plan for a massive armored breakout offensive in Normandy by the British on July 18, 1944.

Operation Roundup   Plan framed in 1942 by General Dwight D. Eisenhower for a 1943 Allied invasion of northern France should there be a Soviet collapse or a sudden weakening of Germany's position.

Overlord   Code name for the 1944 Allied invasion of Normandy, France.

Panzer division   Armored division of the German military.

R.A.F.   Royal Air Force of Great Britain.

Reichsmarshal   Highest rank in Germany's armed forces during World War II; second in rank to German leader and Supreme Commander, Adolf Hitler.

SHAEF   Supreme Headquarters Allied Expeditionary Force; headquarters of the supreme Allied commander in Europe, General Dwight D. Eisenhower, from late 1943 until the end of World War II.

Sword Beach   Code name for one of five designated beaches used during the D-Day landings; beach assigned to the British for the D-Day invasion.

Teheran Conference   Meeting of US president Franklin Delano Roosevelt, British prime minister Winston Churchill, and Soviet premier Joseph Stalin from November 28 to December 1, 1943, in Teheran, Iran, during which they make their first joint declaration against Germany and the other Axis powers.

Utah Beach   Code name for one of five designated beaches used during the D-Day landings; a beach assigned to US forces for the D-Day invasion.

Wehrmacht   Unified German armed forces (army, navy, and air force) before and during World War II.

1939   Britain and France declare war on Germany; World War II begins.

1942   US forces begin to build up in Britain in preparation for D-Day.

1943   The Allies agree at the Casablanca Conference that conditions are not right for D-Day to take place; US president Franklin D. Roosevelt, British prime minister Winston Churchill, and Soviet leader Joseph Stalin meet together for the first time at the Teheran Conference and indicate that May 1944 is the planned date for an Allied landing in France; US general Dwight D. Eisenhower is named Supreme Commander of the Allied Expeditionary Force in Europe; British general Bernard Montgomery is assigned responsibility for the assault landings on D-Day and the following ground fighting.

1944   January: The target date for D-Day is moved from May 1 to May 31; the first amphibious exercise for US troops gets underway in Devon, England.

        April: The British Royal Navy begins to lay mines off German bases along the coast of the English Channel; the overall plan for D-Day is completed; Allied bombers increase raids across northern and western France in preparation for D-Day landings.

        May: D-Day is moved to June 5; the largest series of training exercises—the last before D-Day—take place in southern England; troops that will land in Normandy are sealed in camps along the south coast of England and briefed for D-Day; troops based in England begin their mobilization to cross the English Channel to Normandy.

June 3: Bad weather is predicted for D-Day; US airborne troops are briefed for D-Day.

June 4: The D-Day invasion is postponed due to bad weather and ships already at sea are recalled.

June 5: Eisenhower decides that D-Day will be June 6; British and US airborne troops begin taking off from bases in England.

June 6: D-Day; Battle of Normandy begins.
    12:00 A.M.: British and US airborne paratroopers begin to land in France.
    1:00 A.M.: Landing craft begin to be lowered into the water.
    3:00 A.M.: Gliders begin to reinforce partroopers.
    4:30 A.M.: The Allies liberate the first town in France, Sainte Mère Eglise.
    5:20 A.M.: First bombs are dropped on German targets.
    6:20 A.M.: Allied landing craft approach the beach.
    6:30 A.M.: US troops begin landing at Utah Beach and Omaha Beach.
    7:00 A.M.: German radio broadcasts the first report of the landing.
    7:25 A.M.: British troops begin landing at Sword Beach and Gold Beach.
    7:35 A.M.: Canadian troops begin landing at Juno Beach.
    9:45 A.M.: Utah Beach is cleared of all enemy forces.

12:00 P.M.: Winston Churchill reports on the landings to the British House of Commons.
1:00 P.M.: US troops on Omaha Beach begin moving inland.
12:00 A.M.: D-Day is more or less over.

June 8: British forces liberate Bayeu.

June 12: Carentan is captured.

June 27: US forces liberate Cherbourg.

July: Canadian and British forces liberate Caen; US forces liberate Saint-Lô.

August: The Allies liberate Paris; Battle of Normandy ends.

1945   May 8: VE-Day (Victory in Europe) proclaimed.

August 15: VJ-Day (Victory over Japan) proclaimed.

FOR FURTHER READING

Books

Stephen E. Ambrose, *D-Day, June 6, 1944: The Climatic Battle of World War II*. New York: Simon & Schuster, 1994.

Gerald Astor, *June 6, 1944: The Voices of D-Day*. New York: Dell Publishing, 2002.

Antony Beevor, *D-Day: The Battle for Normandy*. New York: Viking, 2009.

George G. Blackburn, *The Guns of Normandy: A Soldier's Eye View, France 1944*. Toronto: McClelland & Stewart, 1997.

Günther Blumentritt, Wilhelm Keitel, Alfred Jodi, et al, *Fighting the Invasion: The German Army at D-Day*. Ed. David C. Isby. London: Greenhill Books, 2000.

Douglas Brinkley and Ronald J. Drez, *Voices of Valor: D-Day: June 6, 1944*. New York: Bullfinch Press, 2004.

Paul Carrel, *Invasion! They're Coming! The German Account of the D-Day Landings and the 80 Days' Battle for France*. Atglen, PA: Schiffer Publishing, Ltd, 1995.

David G. Chandler and James Lawton Collins Jr., *The D-Day Encyclopedia*. New York: Simon & Schuster, 1994.

Ronald J. Drez, *Remember D-Day: The Plan, the Invasion, Survivor Stories*. Washington, DC: National Geographic, 2004.

Dwight D. Eisenhower, *Crusade in Europe*. Garden City, NY: Doubleday, 1948.

Ken Ford and Steven J. Zaloga, *Overlord: The D-Day Landings*. Oxford, UK: Osprey Publishing Ltd., 2009.

Heniz Guderian, Fritz Kraemer, Fritz Ziegelmann, et al, *Fighting in Normandy: The German Army from D-Day to Villers-Bocage*. Ed. David C. Isby. London: Greenhill Books, 2001.

Tony Hall, ed., *D-Day: Operation Overlord: From the Landing at Normandy to the Liberation of Paris.* New York: Smithmark Publishers Inc., 1993.

Alex Kershaw, *The Bedford Boys: One American Town's Ultimate D-Day Sacrifice.* Cambridge, MA: Da Capo Press, 2003.

Robert J. Kershaw, *D-Day: Piercing the Atlantic Wall.* Annapolis: Naval Institute Press, 1994.

Adrian R. Lewis, *Omaha Beach: A Flawed Victory.* Chapel Hill: The University of North Carolina Press, 2001.

John C. McManus, *The Americans at D-Day: The American Experience at the Normandy Invasion.* New York: Tom Doherty Associates, 2004.

John C. McManus, *The Americans at Normandy: The Summer of 1944—The American War from the Normandy Beaches to Falaise.* New York: Tom Doherty Associates, 2004.

Bernard Montgomery, *The Memoirs of Field-Marshal The Viscount Montgomery of Alamein, K.G.* Cleveland, OH: World Publishing Company, 1958.

Jane Penrose, ed., *The D-Day Companion: Leading Historians Explore History's Greatest Amphibious Assault.* Oxford: Osprey, 2004.

Barrett Tillman, *Brassey's D-Day Encyclopedia: The Normandy Invasion A to Z.* Dulles, VA: Brassey's, 2004.

Peter Tsouras, *Disaster at D-Day: The Germans Defeat the Allies, June 1944.* London: Greenhill Books, 1994.

Periodicals

Thomas B. Allen, "Untold Stories of D-Day," *National Geographic*, June 2002.

John Barry, "Why the Allies Won," *Newsweek*, May 23, 1994.

Timothy B. Benford, "Time to Remember," *World & I*, June 2004.

Charles Cawthon, "D-Day: What It Meant," *American Heritage*, May-June 1994.

Charlie Coon, "D-Day plus 60: German Students' Perspective Is One of Liberation, Not Defeat," *Stars and Stripes*, June 3, 2004.

Alan Cowell, "D-DAY/60 Years Later: For Britain, D-Day Redeemed the Shame of Dunkirk Debacle," *New York Times*, June 8, 2004.

Carlo D'Este, "A Lingering Controversy: Eisenhower's 'Broad Front' Strategy," *Armchair General Magazine*, October 7, 2009.

Carlo D'Este, "Weight of the World," *World War II*, May-June 2010.

Ben Fenton, "Bad Weather Nearly Brought Down D-Day," *Telegraph*, June 5, 2004.

John Keegan, "D-Day," *US News & World Report*, May 23, 1994.

Michael Korda, "1944: Ike's Decision: Eisenhower's Call to Proceed with D-Day Was Anything But Inevitable," *American Heritage*, Winter 2010.

S.L.A. Marshall, "First Wave at Omaha Beach," *Atlantic*, November 1960.

Jeff Nilsson, "The Great Decision: Eisenhower Makes the Call," *Saturday Evening Post*, October 30, 2010.

Richard Overy, "The Normandy Landings: D-Day: An Operation That Filled the British with Dread: Richard Overy, Professor of Modern History at King's College, London, Recounts Churchill's Fears," *Independent*, June 4, 1994.

Michael Paris, "Picturing D-Day," *History Today*, June 2004.

Jonathan Pitts, "Private Heinlein's D-Day: Into the Water, Across the Sand, Under Fire," *Baltimore Sun*, June 4, 2004.

Oleg A. Rzheshevsky, "D-DAY/60 Years Later: For Russia, Opening of a Second Front in Europe Came Far Too Late," *New York Times*, June 8, 2004.

Time, "D-Day," June 6, 1994.

Steve Tuttle, "Tracing Buddy's Footsteps," *Newsweek*, October 16, 2009.

Steve Zaloga, "The Great D-Day," *World War II*, June-July 2008.

Websites

American D-Day (www.americandday.org). This site provides eyewitness accounts, photographs of participants and of activity on the each of the beachheads, after-action reports, journals and war diaries, maps, photos of D-Day commemorative ceremonies, reviews of books on D-Day, and more.

D-Day 60 Years Later (www.time.com). This interactive *Time* magazine site provides video and audio clips, photos of and first person accounts by D-Day veterans, an annotated invasion map, and a special *Life* magazine album of D-Day photos.

D-Day: 60 Years On (www.guardian.co.uk). This site, a Guardian.co.uk special report on D-Day and World War II, provides original *Manchester Guardian* coverage of the landings; recollections of D-Day by British, French, German, US, and Canadian participants and civilians; photos; letters; comments and analysis; and much more.

D-Day June 6, 1944 (www.army.mil/d-day). This official website of the US Army offers a downloadable video of the D-Day landings narrated by veterans who were there. It also provides a collection of US Army photos from the front, descriptions and maps of the Normandy beachheads, invasion-related news articles, and more.

DDay-Overlord.com (www.dday-overlord.com). This site provides comprehensive coverage of D-Day, the Battle of Normandy, and Normandy today. It includes explanations of the various military episodes, operations maps, photos, a listing of D-Day books that can be bought online from the website, a film library with summaries and reviews of D-Day movies and documentaries, and chronologies.

INDEX